Modern Critical Interpretations

The Book of Job

Modern Critical Interpretations

These and other titles in preparation

Modern Critical Interpretations

The Book of Job

Edited and with an introduction by
Harold Bloom
Sterling Professor of the Humanities
Yale University

Chelsea House Publishers ◊ *1988*
NEW YORK ◊ NEW HAVEN ◊ PHILADELPHIA

© 1988 by Chelsea House Publishers,
a division of Chelsea House Educational Communications, Inc.,
   345 Whitney Avenue, New Haven, CT 06511
   95 Madison Avenue, New York, NY 10016
   5068B West Chester Pike, Edgemont, PA 19028

Introduction © 1988 by Harold Bloom

Printed and bound in the United States of America

10 9 8 7 6 5 4 3 2 1

∞ The paper used in this publication meets the minimum
requirements of the American National Standard for Permanence
of Paper for Printed Library Materials, Z39.48–1984.

Library of Congress Cataloging-in-Publication Data
The Book of Job.
   (Modern critical interpretations)
   Bibliography: p.
   Includes index.
   1. Bible. O.T. Job—Criticism, interpretation, etc.
I. Bloom, Harold. II. Series.
BS1415.2.B66 1988   809′.9352231   87–9244
ISBN 0–87754–913–3

Contents

Editor's Note

This book brings together a representative selection of the best modern critical interpretations of the Book of Job. They are reprinted here in the chronological order of their publication. I am grateful to Johann Pillai for his aid in editing this volume.

My introduction argues that the Book of Job is not a theodicy, and balances the interpretive views of Calvin and Kierkegaard against that of Buber. Paul Ricoeur, noted theoretician of reading, analyzes Job's story as a tragic anthropology. In a very different mode, Northrop Frye, anatomist of criticism, expounds William Blake's reading of Job as set forth in the poet-painter's great series of illustrations, which sees Job as being delivered from "natural religion," the Leviathan, by a strenuous act of the imagination.

David Daiches, also rejecting the idea that the Book of Job is a theodicy, concludes that its assault upon God is deliberately subsumed in wonder. In an intricate reading of the book's poetry, Robert Alter demonstrates that there is a dialectical relation between Job's poetry, an instrument for probing his own outrage, and God's poetry, a cosmos of power that transcends Job's predicament.

Job's encounters with the adversary, *ha-satan,* and his own dubious "comforters" are interpreted by Ken Frieden as a complex lesson in a linguistic asceticism that is basic to ancient Judaism. In this book's final essay, René Girard, prophet of sacred violence, examines the agony of Job as scapegoat and powerfully discovers in the Book of Job an ultimate critique of our pernicious refusal to identify ourselves with the victims depicted in our traditions.

Introduction

For Job could not better prove his patience than by resolving to be entirely naked, inasmuch as the good pleasure of God was such. Surely, men resist in vain; they may grit their teeth, but they must return entirely naked to the grave. Even the pagans have said that death alone shows the littleness of men. Why? For we have a gulf of covetousness, that we would wish to gobble up all the earth; if a man has many riches, vines, meadows, and possessions, it is not enough; God would have to create new worlds, if He wished to satisfy us.

JOHN CALVIN, *Second Sermon on Job*

And yet there is no hiding place in the wide world where troubles may not find you, and there has never lived a man who was able to say more than you can say, that you do not know when sorrow will visit your house. So be sincere with yourself, fix your eyes upon Job; even though he terrifies you, it is not this he wishes, if you yourself do not wish it.

SØREN KIERKEGAARD, *Edifying Discourses*

The poet of Job emulates a strong precursor, that astonishing prophet, Jeremiah. Though the Book of Job is less shocking, rhetorically and dialectically, than Jeremiah's book, it remains profoundly troubling. Like *King Lear,* which is manifestly influenced by it, the Book of Job touches the limits of literature and perhaps transcends them. Lear desperately prays for patience, lest he go mad, and even declares, "No, I will be the pattern of all patience, / I will say nothing," as though he would be a second Job. In the play's greatest scene (4.6), perhaps the finest in Shakespeare or in literature, Lear advises Gloucester to join him in the Jobean fortitude:

> If thou wilt weep my fortunes, take my eyes.
> I know thee well enough, thy name is Gloucester.

> Thou must be patient; we came crying hither.
> Thou know'st, the first time that we smell the air
> We wawl and cry.

Patient Job is actually about as patient as Lear is. *Ha-satan,* the adversary, is provocative enough, but Job's comforters are worse. William Blake bitterly wrote that "in the Book of Job, Milton's Messiah is call'd Satan," and clearly Job's abominable friends are what *The Marriage of Heaven and Hell* calls "Angels," or pious time-servers, fit to become minor officials of Kafka's court or Kafka's castle. Despite pious tamperings, such as the absurd epilogue, the Book of Job is not the work of a trimmer or of a self-deceived saint. Its best expositors remain two fierce Protestants, John Calvin and Søren Kierkegaard. Calvin condemns us for not being Jobean enough:

> Meanwhile God will be condemned among us. This is how men exasperate themselves. And in this what do they do? It is as if they accuse God of being a tyrant or a hairbrain who asked only to put everything in confusion.

Kierkegaard exalts Job as a hero of the spirit, a champion who has overcome the world:

> But he who sees God has overcome the world, and therefore Job in his devout word had overcome the world; was through his devout word greater and stronger and more powerful than the whole world, which here would not so much carry him into temptation but would overcome him with its power, cause him to sink down before its boundless might.

I take from Calvin his accurate sense that Job does not condemn God, does not accuse him of being "a tyrant or a hairbrain." From Kierkegaard, I take his realization that it is not the Behemoth or the Leviathan that causes Job to sink down when God comes at last to confront the sufferer and speaks out of the whirlwind to him. Martin Buber shrewdly notes that "Job cannot forego either his own truth or God." Protesting the incommensurable, suffering far in excess of sin, Job is answered by a God who speaks only in terms of the incommensurable. Like Jeremiah, the poet of Job returns to the J writer or Yahwist whose Yahweh is uncanny. We are made in Yahweh's image and are asked to be like him, but we are not to presume to be too much like him. He can be argued with, as when Abraham argues him part way down on the road to Sodom, but he also is subject to peculiar vagaries, as when he tries to murder poor Moses at the outset of the prophet's reluctant mission or when he alternately entices and warns the people on Sinai. I take it that Job recognizes the reality of Yahweh's extraordinary personality after the voice out of the whirlwind has completed its message, a recognition that is the resolution of the book.

It seems clear to me that the Book of Job is not a theodicy, a justification of the ways of God to man, as Milton defines the genre in his sublime theodicy, *Paradise Lost.* The voice out of the whirlwind does not seek to justify. Rather, with an ultimate exuberance, it bombards Job with a great series of rhetorical questions, which attain their summit in the vision of the Leviathan:

> Canst thou draw out leviathan with an hook? or his tongue with a cord *which* thou lettest down?
>
> 2 Canst thou put an hook into his nose? or bore his jaw through with a thorn?
>
> 3 Will he make many supplications unto thee? will he speak soft *words* unto thee?
>
> 4 Will he make a covenant with thee? wilt thou take him for a servant for ever?
>
> 5 Wilt thou play with him as *with* a bird? or wilt thou bind him for thy maidens?
>
> 6 Shall the companions make a banquet of him? shall they part him among the merchants?
>
> 7 Canst thou fill his skin with barbed irons? or his head with fish spears?
>
> 8 Lay thine hand upon him, remember the battle, do no more.
>
> 9 Behold, the hope of him is in vain: shall not *one* be cast down even at the sight of him?
>
> 10 None *is so* fierce that dare stir him up: who then is able to stand before me?

Ahab's answer in *Moby-Dick* was a fierce affirmative until his life ended with his outcry "*Thus,* I give up the spear!" as he rammed his harpoon vainly into the White Whale's sanctified flesh. Job is no Ahab, nor an apocalyptic seer. But it is difficult not to prefer Ahab to Job, when God taunts us with such vicious irony: "Will he make a covenant with thee?" In Kabbalistic prophecy, the companions do make a banquet of the Leviathan when the Messiah comes, but Job is no Kabbalist. The Book of Job is the strong, implicit opponent of that belated doctrine Gnosticism, and nothing could be further from Job than the Lurianic doctrine of the breaking of the primal vessels of creation.

Confronted by the Leviathan, Job declares that he had lacked knowledge:

> therefore have I uttered that I understood not; things too wonderful for me, which I knew not.

The Hebrew text does not say "things too wonderful for me" but "things beyond me." Confronting the sublimity of Yahweh, Job understands his own tradition, which is that the sage must rise to the agon, as Abraham and Jacob did, and so behave pragmatically as if he were everything in himself while knowing always that, in relation to Yahweh, he is nothing in himself. Job prefigures Martin Buber's theological vision: the "eclipse" of God. God's answer, out of the whirlwind, is read by Buber as being "not *the* divine justice, which remains hidden, but *a* divine justice, namely that manifest in creation." Buber cites Rudolf Otto here on the playful riddle of God's creative power. Karl Barth in his *Church Dogmatics* makes a nice point illuminating this riddle, which is that God shrewdly allows creation to speak for him:

> He obviously counts upon it that they belong so totally to Him, that they are so subject to Him and at His disposal, that in speaking of themselves they will necessarily speak of Him.

Like Rudolf Otto and Karl Barth, Martin Buber sees Job as a "faithful rebel" and so as a servant of God. All three men of God seem to fall short of the Book of Job's bitter ironies, which is why I prefer the answering irony of John Calvin, "God would have to create new worlds, if He wished to satisfy us," or the more complex irony of Kierkegaard, "Fix your eyes upon Job; even though he terrifies you, it is not this he wishes, if you yourself do not wish it." We cannot be satisfied, because Yahweh will create no more new worlds, and we need to be terrified by Job, even if he does not will to terrify us. The limits of desire are also the limits of literature. Kierkegaard is singularly perceptive; it is not the creation but the creator who overwhelms

Job. Our desires for the good are incommensurate not with the good but with the creator of good. Shelley, in the accents of Gnosticism, declared that good and the means of good were irreconcilable. Job, in the accents of Jeremiah, accepted his election of adversity.

The Reaffirmation of the Tragic

Paul Ricoeur

Let us . . . sketch the movement that leads from the Adamic myth to the tragic myth under its two aspects, anthropological and theological, and from the tragic myth to the most archaic and apparently most outmoded vision of the world, the vision of theogony.

The Adamic myth is anti-tragic; that is clear. The fated aberration of man, the indivisibility of the guilt of the hero and the guilt of the wicked god are no longer thinkable after the twofold confession, in the Augustinian sense of the word confession, of the holiness of God and the sin of man. And yet the Adamic myth does reaffirm something of the tragic man and even something of the tragic god.

There are several "tragic" aspects of the Adamic myth. We have hinted [elsewhere] at the "tragic" meaning of the figure of the serpent, which is *already* there and *already* evil. But before coming back to the serpent, we must note the tragic accent of the Adamic figure itself. That figure thematizes a mystery of iniquity which is not reducible to the clear consciousness of actual evil, of the evil beginning in the instant; it points towards an underlying *peccability* which, as Kierkegaard says in *The Concept of Dread,* endures and increases quantitatively. That underlying peccability is like the horizon of actual evil, and is perceived only as horizon, at the frontier of the avowal of present evil. Later speculation will endeavor to fix that underlying peccability in the false concept of inheritance. The rationalization of original sin as inherited sin was to encumber Western thought for centuries. It is necessary

From *The Symbolism of Evil.* © 1967 by Paul Ricoeur. Harper & Row, 1967.

to undo this knot of speculation and to display the motivations deposited as a sediment in the pseudo-thought of an original sin which was supposed to be both a *first* sin and a *transmitted* heritage; it is necessary to come back to the limiting concept of an evil concerning which I confess that it is already there in the very instant in which I avow that I put it there. This other side, not posited, of an evil that is posited, is the "radical" in radical evil; but I know it only as implied.

The other myths speak of the anteriority (theogonic myth) of this reverse side of sin, the sin committed by all men in Adam, or of its passiveness and externality (Orphic myth), or, finally, of its fatedness, which is the contribution of the tragic myth. By means of an unavowable theology, aspects of the Ineluctable are made manifest which are not opposed to freedom, but are implied by it, and which cannot be made the objects of biological, psychological, or sociological knowledge, but are accessible only to symbolic and mythical expression. It is precisely the tragic myth which is the depository of the Ineluctable implied in the very exercise of freedom, and which awakens us to those fateful aspects which we are always stirring up and uncovering as we progress in maturity, autonomy, and the social engagement of our freedom. The myth regroups these fateful aspects, which come to the surface discontinuously through scattered signs. For example, it is not possible for me to aim at completeness without running the risk of losing myself in the indefinitely varied abundance of experience or in the niggardly narrowness of a perspective as restricted as it is consistent. Between chaos and the void, between ruinous wealth and destructive impoverishment, I must make my way by a road that is difficult and, in certain respects, impossible. It is Ineluctable that I lose the wealth in order to have unity, and vice versa. Kierkegaard clearly recognized the incompossibility of the requirements for becoming oneself; *The Concept of Dread* evokes the two ways in which a man may lose himself: in the infinite without finiteness or in the finite without infinity, in reality without possibility or in imagination without the efficacy of work, marriage, profession, political activity.

To this major sign of the fateful character of freedom many others can be added. Who can realize himself without excluding not only possibilities but realities and existences, and, consequently, without destroying? Who can join the intensity of friendship and love to the breadth of universal solidarity? It is a tragic aspect of existence that the history of self-awareness cannot begin with the sympathy of the Stoics, but must start with the struggle of master and slave, and that, once having consented to itself and to the universal, it must plunge anew into self-division.

Now, all these fateful aspects, because they are implied in freedom and not opposed to it, are necessarily experienced as fault. It is I who raise up the Ineluctable, within myself and outside myself, in developing my existence. Here, then, is a fault no longer in an ethical sense, in the sense of a transgression of the moral law, but in an existential sense: to become oneself is to fail to realize wholeness, which nevertheless remains the end, the dream, the horizon, and that which the Idea of happiness points to. Because fate belongs to freedom as the nonchosen portion of all our choices, it must be experienced as fault.

Thus the tragic myth is reaffirmed as an associated myth, revealing the fateful reverse side of the ethical confession of sins. Under the figure of the blinded and misled hero, it expresses the role of ineluctable guilt. This fateful aspect, joined to the aspects of antecedence and externality expressed by the other myths, points toward the quasi-nature of an evil already there, at the very heart of the evil that springs up now. It can only be represented dramatically, theatrically, as a "fate," as a fold or crease that freedom has contracted. That is why tragedy survived its destruction by Platonism and Christianity. What cannot be thought, can and must nevertheless be exhibited in the figure of the tragic hero; and that figure necessarily excites anew the great tragic emotions; for the nonposited aspect that any positing of evil involves can only awaken terror and compassion, beyond all judgment and all condemnation; a *merciful* vision of man comes to limit the accusation and save him from the wrath of the Judge.

It is here that the "tragic" light cast upon the Adamic myth enhances the enigma of the serpent. As we have said [elsewhere], it is not possible to absorb all the meanings revealed through that figure into the avowal of a purely human origin of evil. The serpent is more than the transcendence of sin over sins, more than the nonposited of the posited, more than the radical of radical evil; it is the Other, it is the Adversary, the pole of a counterparticipation, of a counterlikeness, about which one can say nothing except that the evil act, in positing itself, *lets itself be seduced* by the counterpositing of a source of iniquity represented by the Evil One, the Diabolical. When tragedy *shows* the hero blinded by a demonic power, it manifests the demonic side of the human experience of evil by means of the tragic action; it makes visible, without ever making it thinkable, the situation of the wicked who can never occupy any but the second place in wickedness, "after" the Adversary. Thus, the tragic *representation* continues to express not only the *reverse side* of all confession of sins, but the *other pole* of human evil; the evil for which I assume responsibility makes manifest a source of evil for which I cannot assume responsibility, but which I participate in every time that through me evil enters into the world as if for the first time. It might be said that the avowal of evil as human calls forth a second-degree avowal, that of evil as nonhuman. Only tragedy can accept this avowal of the avowal and exhibit it in a spectacle, for no coherent discourse can include that Other.

But perhaps there is more to be said: it is not only something of the tragic anthropology that is reaffirmed by the Adamic myth, but something even of the tragic theology. The tragic element in biblical theology can be discovered in the following way. I will start with the *ethical* sense to which the Covenant between Israel and Yahweh was elevated. That ethical sense, which makes the Law the bond between man and God, reacts upon the conception of God himself; God is an ethical God. This "ethicization" of man and God tends toward a moral vision of the world, according to which History is a tribunal, pleasures and pains are retribution, God himself is a judge. At the same time, the whole of human experience assumes a penal character. Now, this moral vision of the world was wrecked by Jewish thought itself, when it meditated on the suffering of the innocent. The book of Job is the upsetting document that records this shattering of the moral vision of the world. The figure of Job bears witness to the irreducibility of the evil of scandal to the evil of fault, at least on the scale of human experience; the theory of retribution, which was the first, naive expression of the moral vision of the world, does not account for all the unhappiness in the world. Hence, it may be asked whether the Hebrew and, more generally, the Near Eastern theme of the "suffering Just One" does not lead back from the prophetic *accusation* to tragic *pity*.

The movement of thought that we shall try to describe rests on the ethical vision itself: where God is perceived as the origin of justice and the source of legislation, the problem of just sanctions is raised with a seriousness without precedent; suffering emerges as an enigma when the demands of justice can no longer explain it; this enigma is the product of the ethical theology itself. That is why the virulence of the book of Job is without equivalent in any culture; Job's complaint supposes the full maturity of an ethical vision of God; the clearer God becomes as legislator, the more obscure he becomes as creator; the irrationality of power balances the ethical rationalization of holiness; it becomes possible to turn the accusation back against God, against the ethical God of the accusation. Thereupon there begins the foolish business of trying to justify God: theodicy is born.

It is at this point of doubt, when the spontaneous ethical vision appeals to the arguments of theodicy and has recourse to a rhetoric of conviction, that the possibility of a tragic vision looms up again. That possibility is born of the impossibility of saving the ethical vision with the aid of any "proof." The friends of Job do, indeed, mobilize forgotten sins, unknown sins, ancestral sins, the sins of the people, in order to restore the equation of suffering and punishment; but Job refuses to close the gap. His innocence and his suffering are marginal to any ethical vision. (There is no need to ask whether such a just man existed, nor even whether such a just man is possible. Job is the *imaginary* personage who serves as touchstone for the ethical vision of the world and makes it fly to pieces. By hypothesis or by construction, Job is innocent; he must be just in order that the problem may be posed in all its intensity: how is it possible that a man so wholly just should be so totally suffering? Besides, such a product of the imagination was made possible precisely by the attainment of the idea of *degrees* of guilt; the imagining of the extremes of the just and the unjust is enveloped in the representation of gradual guilt; Job is the zero degree of guilt joined to the extreme of suffering; from this conjunction is born the scandal which also is extreme.)

Babylonian "wisdom" had already carried very far the dissolution that the ethical vision suffers when it comes into contact with meditation on suffering. For the author of *A Pessimistic Dialogue between Master and Servant* [an ancient Babylonian text], suffering is not so much unjust as senseless, and it has the result of making every undertaking senseless; in the face of absurdity, everything is equal. Thus the ethical vision is eaten away right down to the very core of action. In other texts, such as the poem of the suffering just man ("I Will Praise the Lord of Wisdom"), complaint is pushed to such a point of despair that it rivals Job's complaint and protestation, but "wisdom" counsels mute resignation and a most extreme sacrifice of the will to know; a theophany of Marduk, which fills the believer with gratitude, but not with understanding, casts a ray of hope into the darkness of distress.

Scepticism, surrender to the inscrutable, modest hedonism, expectation of a miracle—all these attitudes are already held in reserve and in suspense in the Babylonian "wisdom." The complainer, then, will sacrifice his complaint, will learn patience, will surrender himself humbly into the hands of an inscrutable god, and will forgo knowledge.

But the most extraordinary document of the ancient "wisdom" of the Near East, concerning the turn from ethical comprehension to tragic comprehension of God himself, is the book of Job. And since the "ethicization" of the divine had nowhere else been carried as far as in Israel, the *crisis* of that vision of the world was nowhere else as radical. Only the protestation of *Prometheus Bound* can perhaps be compared with that of Job; but the Zeus that Prometheus calls in question is not the holy God of the Prophets. To recover the hyperethical dimension of God, it was necessary that the alleged justice of the law of retribution should be turned against God and that God should appear unjustifiable from the point of view of the scheme of justification that had guided the whole process of "ethicization." Hence the tone of legal pleading in the book, which turns against the earlier theodicy invoked by the three "friends."

> I know as much as you; I yield to you in nothing.
> But I must speak to Shaddai;
> I wish to remonstrate with God. . . .
> He may slay me: I have no other hope
> than to justify my conduct before him.
>
> (13:2–3, 15)

> Oh! if I knew how to find him,
>   how to come to his dwelling place,
> I would present my case before him,
>   my mouth would be full of arguments.
> I would know the words of his defense,
>   I would be attentive to what he would say to me.
>
> (23:3–5)

Job's admirable apology in chapter 31—which is also an interesting document concerning the scrupulous conscience, in virtue of its enumeration of the faults that Job has not committed—ends with these proud words:

> Oh! who will make God listen to me?
> I have said my last word; let Shaddai answer me!
> If my adversary will write out an indictment,
> I will wear it upon my shoulder,
> I will put it on like a diadem.
>
> (31:35–36)

The putting in question of the ethical God reaches its utmost virulence when it begins to disturb the dialogal situation which, in Israel, is at the very basis of the consciousness of sin. Man is before God as before his aggressor and his enemy. The eye of God, which represented for Israel the absolute measure of sin, as well as the watchfulness and the compassion of the Lord, becomes a source of terror:

> What is man, that you make so much of him,
>   that you fix your attention on him,
> that you inspect him every morning,
>   that you scrutinize him every instant?
> Will you ever stop looking at me
>   for the length of time it takes to swallow my spittle?
>
> (7:17–19)

The eye of God is upon Job as the eye of the hunter is upon the wild beast; God "surrounds" him, God "spies on" him, he "encompasses him with his nets," he ravages his house and "exhausts his strength." Job goes so far as to suspect that it is that inquisitorial eye which makes man guilty: "Yes, I know that it is so; but how shall a man be just before God?" On the contrary, is not man too *weak* for God to require so much of him? "Will you frighten a leaf that is driven by the wind, or pursue a dry straw?" (13:25).

> Man born of woman,
>   short-lived, but with more than enough troubles.
>   Like a flower, he opens and then fades,
>   he flees like a shadow without stopping.
> And you deign to open your eyes upon him,
>   you bring him into judgment before you!
>
> (14:1–3)

Then Job cursed the day of his birth: "Let the day perish wherein I was born, and the night in which it was said: A man child has been conceived! . . . Why did I not die from the womb? Why did I not perish as soon as I was born?" (3:3, 11).

> My hope is to inhabit Sheol,
>   to make my bed in the darkness.
> I cry to the grave: "You are my father!"
>   to the vermin: "You are my mother and my sister!"
>
> (17:13–14)

Faced with the torturing absence of God (23:8; 30:20), the man dreams of his own absence and repose:

> Henceforth I shall be invisible to every eye;
>   your eyes will be upon me and I shall have vanished.
>
> (7:8)

Is it not the tragic God that Job discovers again? the inscrutable God of terror? What is tragic, too, is the dénouement. "Suffering for the purpose of understanding," the Greek chorus said. Job, in his turn, penetrates beyond any ethical vision to a new dimension of faith, the dimension of *unverifiable* faith.

We must never lose sight of the fact that Job's plaint, even when it seems to be destroying the basis of any dialogal relation between God and man, does not cease to move in the field of invocation. It is to God that Job appeals against God:

> Oh! that you would hide me in Sheol,
>   that you would shelter me there, until your anger passes,
> that you would fix a time for me and remember me thereafter:
>   —for, once dead, can a man come to life again?—
> All the days of my service I would wait
>   for my relief to come.
>
> (14:13–14)

"Even now I have a witness in heaven, and my defender is on high" (16:19). . . . "I know that my defender is living, and that at the end he will rise upon the earth. After my awakening, he will raise me up beside him and in my flesh I shall see God" (19:25–26).

This faith gets its veracity from the very defiance that argues against the vain science of retribution and renounces the wisdom that is inaccessible to man (chap. 28). In his unknowing, Job alone has "spoken rightly" of God (42:7).

Shall we say that Job returns to the crushing silence of resignation, like the Babylonian Job? Yes, up to a certain point. The God who answers Job "out of the storm" reverses the relation of questioner and questioned: "Where were you when I laid the foundations of the earth? Speak, if your knowledge is enlightened" (38:4). "Gird up your loins like a man. I am going to question you, and you will give me the answers" (40:7). And Job gave this answer to Yahweh:

I know that you are all-powerful;
   what you plan, you can accomplish.
It was I who darkened your counsels
   by utterances without sense.
Therefore I have spoken without understanding,
   concerning things too wonderful for me, about which I know
   nothing.
(Listen, let me speak,
   I am going to question you and you will give me the answers.)
I did not know you except by hearsay,
   but now my eyes have seen you.
Therefore I take back my words,
   I repent in dust and ashes.

(42:2–6)

   And yet the silence of Job, once the question itself has been blasted
by the lightning, is not altogether the seal of meaninglessness. Neither
is it altogether the zero degree of speech. Certain words are addressed
to Job in exchange for his silence. Those words are not an answer to
his problem; they are not at all a solution of the problem of suffering;
they are in no way a reconstruction, at a higher degree of subtlety, of
the ethical vision of the world. The God who addresses Job out of the
tempest shows him Behemoth and Leviathan, the hippopotamus and
the crocodile, vestiges of the chaos that has been overcome, representing a brutality dominated and measured by the creative act. Through
these symbols he gives him to understand that all is order, measure,
and beauty—inscrutable order, measure beyond measure, terrible beauty.
A way is marked out between agnosticism and the penal view of
history and life—the way of unverifiable faith. There is nothing in that
revelation that concerns him personally; but precisely because it is not
a question of himself, Job is challenged. The oriental poet, like
Anaximander and Heraclitus the Obscure, announces an order beyond
order, a totality full of meaning, within which the individual must lay
down his recrimination. Suffering is not explained, ethically or otherwise; but the contemplation of the whole initiates a movement which
must be completed practically by the surrender of a claim, by the
sacrifice of the demand that was at the beginning of the recrimination,
namely, the claim to form by oneself a little island of meaning in the
universe, an empire within an empire. It becomes suddenly apparent

that the demand for retribution animated Job's recriminations no less than the moralizing homilies of his friends. That, perhaps, is why the innocent Job, the upright Job, repents. Of what can he repent, if not of his claim for compensation, which made his contention impure? Was it not still the law of retribution which drove him to demand an explanation in proportion to his existence, a private explanation, a finite explanation?

As in tragedy, the final theophany has explained nothing to him, but it has changed his view; he is ready to identify his freedom with inimical necessity; he is ready to convert freedom and necessity into fate. This conversion is the true "reenactment"—no longer the material reenactment which is still a kind of recompense and hence a sort of retribution, but the wholly internal reenactment which is no longer restoration of an earlier happiness, but reenactment of the present unhappiness.

I do not mean to say that all this is already in the book of Job. But that is how we can bring it to completion in ourselves, starting from the impulse that we receive from it. That impulse is given by a simple touch in the prologue: Satan has made a bet that Job, if he is confronted with misfortune, will not fear God "for nothing" (1:9). This is what is at stake: to renounce the law of retribution to the extent not only of ceasing to envy the prosperity of the wicked, but of enduring misfortune as one accepts good fortune—that is to say, as God-given (2:10). Such is the tragic wisdom of the "reenactment" that triumphs over the ethical vision of the world.

If now we turn back from "faith in the hidden God" and the "reenactment" of misfortune—which illuminates it with a sombre light—to the Adamic myth, we see what tragedy contributes to the understanding of that myth. It contributes two things: on the one hand, pity for human beings, who are nevertheless accused by the Prophet; on the other hand, fear and trembling before the divine abyss, before the God whose holiness is nevertheless proclaimed by the Prophet. Perhaps it is necessary that the possibility of the tragic God should never be abolished altogether, so that biblical theology may be protected from the platitudes of ethical monotheism, with its Legislator and its Judge, confronting a moral subject who is endowed with complete and unfettered freedom, still intact after each act. Because the tragic theology is always possible, although not to be spoken, God is *Deus Absconditus*. And it is always possible, because suffering can no longer be understood as a chastisement.

Just as the tragic anthropology regroups the scattered signs of the ineluctable that are mingled with the growth of our concrete freedom, so the tragic theology regroups with signs of the apparent hostility of fate. Those signs appear when, for example, our vision of things becomes contracted. When wholeness is lost, we sink into the singularity of conclusions without premises. Only the "seer" of Greek tragedy and the "fool" of Shakespearian tragedy escape from the tragic; the seer and the fool have ascended from the tragic to the comic by their access to a comprehensive vision. Now, nothing is more likely to destroy that comprehensive vision than suffering. We are still close to the tragic theology when the contradiction seems to us not only unresolved but unresolvable. A nondialectical contradiction; there we have the tragic. Thus Antigone and Creon destroy one another, and there is no third force that might mediate their opposition and embrace the good reasons of both. That a value cannot be realized without the destruction of another value, equally positive—there, again, is the tragic. It is perhaps at its height when it seems that the furthering of a value requires the destruction of its bearer. It seems then that it is the very nature of things that makes such a thing happen; the very order of the world becomes a temptation to despair. "The object in the background of the tragic," says Max Scheler, "is always the world itself, thought of as a unity—the world in which such a thing is possible." The indifference of the course of events to human values, the *blind* character of necessity—of the sun that shines on the good and the bad—play the role of the Greek μοῖρα, which becomes a κακὸς δαίμων, as soon as value-relations and personal relations are confronted with relations of the causal order. The hero is the point of intersection, the "tragic knot," as Max Scheler also says, where the blindness of order is transformed into the enmity in fate; the tragic is always personal, but it makes manifest a sort of cosmic sadness which reflects the hostile transcendence to which the hero is a prey. And since the hero is the agent of that apparent enmity in the principle of things, since he "delays" the progress and "precipitates" the dénouement of the tragic action, blind necessity appears to be a hostile intention intertwined with the intention of the tragic hero.

That is why the tragic vision always remains possible, resisting any logical, moral, or aesthetic reconciliation.

Shall we leave the Adamic myth and the tragic myth face to face, as two interpretations of existence between which we can only fluctuate endlessly? Not at all.

In the first place, the tragic myth saves the biblical myth only insofar as the latter first resuscitates it. We must not grow weary of repeating that only he who confesses that he is the author of evil discovers the reverse of that confession, namely, the *nonposited* in the positing of evil, the always *already* there of evil, the *other* of temptation, and finally the incomprehensibility of God, who tests me and who can appear to me as my enemy. In this circular relation between the Adamic myth and the tragic myth, the Adamic myth is the right side and the tragic myth is the reverse side.

But, above all, the polarity of the two myths betokens the arrest of understanding at a certain stage. At that stage our vision remains dichotomous. On the one hand, the evil that is *committed* leads to a just exile; that is what the figure of Adam represents. On the other hand, the evil that is *suffered* leads to an unjust deprivation; that is what the figure of Job represents. The first figure calls for the second; the second corrects the first. Only a third figure could announce the transcending of the contradiction, and that would be the figure of the "Suffering Servant," who would make of suffering, of the evil that is undergone, an *action* capable of redeeming the evil that is committed. This enigmatic figure is the one celebrated by the Second Isaiah in the four "songs of the Servant of Yahweh" (Isa. 42:1–9; 49:1–6; 50:4–11; 52:13–53:12), and it opens up a perspective radically different from that of "wisdom." It is not contemplation of creation and its immense measure that consoles; it is suffering itself. Suffering has become a gift that expiates the sins of the people.

> It was our sufferings that he bore
> and our griefs with which he was laden.
> And we thought of him as chastised,
> stricken by God, and humiliated.
> He was pierced for our sins,
> crushed for our crimes.
> The chastisement that brings us peace is upon him
> and it is owing to his wounds that we are healed.
>
> . . . .
>
> Yes, he was cut off from the land of the living
> for our sins, he was smitten to death.
>
> (Isa. 53:4–5, 8b)

Whatever may be the meaning of this "Suffering Servant," whether he be a historical personage, individual or collective, or the figure of a Savior to come, he reveals an entirely new possibility—that suffering gives itself a meaning, by voluntary consent, in the meaninglessness of scandal. In the juridical and penal view of life, guilt had to provide the reason for suffering. But the suffering of the innocent broke the schema of retribution in pieces; sin and suffering are separated by an abyss of irrationality. It is then that the suffering of the "Suffering Servant" institutes a bond between suffering and sin, at another level than that of retribution. But the tragedy of the "Suffering Servant" is beyond the Greek tragedy of the hero.

Of course, there is no lack of "juridical theologies," which have understood substitutive suffering as a supreme way of salvaging the law of retribution. According to that schema, the suffering which is a gift would be the means by which mercy would give "satisfaction" to justice. In this mechanical balancing of the divine attributes, justice and mercy, the new quality of the offered suffering is swallowed up again in the quantitative law of retribution. In truth, the suffering that is a gift takes up into itself the suffering that is a scandal, and thus inverts the relation of guilt to suffering. According to the old law, guilt was supposed to produce suffering as a punishment; but now a suffering that is *outside* retribution, a senseless and scandalous suffering, anticipates human evil and takes upon itself the sins of the world. There had to appear a suffering which would free itself from the legal-mindedness of retribution and submit voluntarily to the iron law, in order to suppress it by fulfilling it. In short, a stage of absurd suffering, the stage of Job, was needed, to mediate the movement from punishment to generosity. But then guilt gets a new horizon: not that of Judgment, but that of Mercy.

What does the tragic vision signify with respect to this ultimate significance of suffering? The tragic vision always remains possible for all of us who have not attained the capacity for offered suffering. Short of this holiness of suffering, the question remains: Is not God wicked? Is it not that possibility that the believer evokes when he prays: "Lead us not into temptation"? Does not his request signify: "Do not come to meet me with the face of the tragic God"? There is a theology of temptation which is very close to the tragic theology of blinding. . . .

That is why tragedy has never finished dying. Killed twice, by the philosophical Logos and by the Judeo-Christian Kerygma, it survived its double death. The theme of the wrath of God, the ultimate motive of the tragic consciousness, is invincible to the arguments of the philosopher as well as of the theologian. For there is no rational vindication of the innocence of God; every explanation of the Stoic or

Leibnizian type is wrecked, like the naive arguments of Job's friends, on the suffering of the innocent. They leave intact the opacity of evil and the opacity of the world "in which such a thing is possible," as Max Scheler says in his essay on the "Phenomenon of the Tragic"; as soon as meaninglessness appears to swoop down intentionally on man, the schema of the wrath of God looms up and the tragic consciousness is restored. Only a consciousness that had accepted suffering without reservation could also begin to absorb the Wrath of God into the Love of God; but even then the suffering of others, the suffering of children, of the lowly, would renew the mystery of iniquity in his eyes. Only *timid* hope could anticipate in silence the end of the phantasm of the "wicked God."

Blake's Reading of the Book of Job

Northrop Frye

For all the discussion that there has been over Blake's illustrations to the Book of Job, . . . there is perhaps still room for more consideration of how Blake read the book. Everyone realizes that Blake re-created the book in his engravings, and was not simply illustrating it. At the same time he appears to be following it with considerable fidelity, and his attitude toward it, in striking contrast to his attitude toward the original of the other great work of his last period, the illustrations to Dante's *Commedia,* seems to be on the whole an attitude of critical acceptance. He remarked, apropos of Homer, that "Every Poem must necessarily be a perfect Unity," but that the *Iliad* is not "peculiarly so," which implies that the perfect unity is potential in the poem itself, and is really achieved by the reader. The sense of unity that one feels about the Job engravings, considered as a series, indicates that Blake extracted a corresponding unity out of his text.

This fact is more complicated than it looks, because despite the Book of Job's formidable literary reputation, it is not easy to see how its argument makes a sense congenial to Blake. It begins with the astonishing scenes of Satan in the court of God, where Satan has the role, always central to his nature for Blake, of the accuser of mankind. He suggests that God has set things up in such a way that he can't lose: if he rewards obedience, he gives man so powerful a motive for being obedient that the service of God becomes a conditioned reflex. He may

From *Spiritus Mundi: Essays on Literature, Myth, and Society.* © 1976 by Indiana University Press.

be raising the issue of man's free will, but not in a way that could ever help man to become free. Later in the poem, Job's three friends keep revolving around the central pseudo-problem of the righteousness of God's ways. Those who do well will be rewarded and those who do evil will be punished; therefore it must be a crime to be unfortunate. If it were not, God would not be a just God. The suppressed premise here is that God administers both the human moral law and the physical natural law, but it never occurs to them to doubt this. Blake doubts it, however: it is the basis of what he repudiates as natural religion.

The friends' view of providence is easily refuted by experience, but when it is, they can give two possible answers. One is to say that God's ways are inscrutable, although they seem to the unprejudiced reader to be merely insane on such premises. The other is to assume that God's providence will manifest itself in another world, from which no evidence ever leaks out. If it appears that "honesty is the best policy" is nonsense, the argument shifts to "maybe it doesn't seem so now, but you just wait."

The arguments of the three friends reach a deadlock, and Elihu takes over, to overwhelm Job with the eloquence of what he has to say "on God's behalf" (36:2), but although his eloquence is genuine enough, he is concerned mostly with restating the earlier arguments. When God himself answers Job out of the whirlwind and asks "Who is this that darkeneth counsel by words without knowledge?" (38:2), apparently meaning Elihu, we expect the definitive revelation to which the whole drama seems to have been leading up. But we feel uncomfortable about the way in which God triumphantly displays a number of trump cards that seem to belong to a different game. He asks Job a series of rhetorical questions which have a hectoring and bullying sound to them. Were you around when I made the world, or do you understand all about how it was made? No? Well, then, why are you raising doubts about my administrative competence? This is followed by poems on the two beasts Behemoth and Leviathan—remarkable poems, but we wonder about their relevance to Job's boils and murdered children. Job replies meekly that he has "uttered that I understood not; things too wonderful for me which I knew not . . . wherefore I abhor myself, and repent in dust and ashes" (42:3–6). God then appears to say, in effect, "Well, that's better," and forthwith restores Job to prosperity. Job's friends and their natural religion, apparently, have really been right all along, even though they are said not to be.

Somehow it does not sound like the kind of argument that Blake would regard with much favor.

The Book of Job is technically a comedy by virtue of Job's restoration in the last few verses, but the comic conclusion seems so wrenched and arbitrary that it is hard to think of it as anything but a wantonly spoiled tragedy. In all the gropings that Job and the three friends and Elihu all make after some explanation for Job's plight, one explanation that they never speculate about is the one that has already been given to the reader. It never occurs to them that God might have deliberately exposed Job to such an ordeal in order to win a wager with Satan. They are all, including Job himself, far too pious and sincere for such a notion ever to occur to them. The prologue in heaven hangs sardonically over the whole debate, and we wait for God to reveal to Job something of what the reader knows. But not a word is said about Satan at the end of the action, and Job learns nothing about the original compact. The simplest answer is to suppose that the Book of Job, begun by a colossal poetic genius, fell into the hands of a superstitious editor whose attitude was a cruder version of that of Job's friends, and who twisted one of the world's profoundest poems into an obscurantist tirade against the use of the questioning intelligence. Something like this could have happened: there are signs of nervous editing, as in so many parts of the Bible, and it is impossible to say how far expurgation has gone. But such a hypothesis is of no use to us: the version we have is the only one that has influenced later literature and religion, and the only one that Blake read. He must have read it, however, in a way very different from the summary of it just given.

First of all, the comic conclusion, the restoring of Job to prosperity, would not have seemed arbitrary to Blake, but inevitable. The Bible as a whole takes the form of a U-shaped narrative in which Adam loses his garden and is led back, at the end of time, to a restored garden which is also a city. This means, according to Milton, that he loses paradise as a physical environment and regains it as an inner state of mind. The latter, Michael tells Adam in *Paradise Lost,* is "happier far" than the original Eden. Blake would have seen the story of Job as an epitome of the biblical narrative, in which the final restoration provides a greater happiness than the original state. As Blake sees the story, Job begins in the state of Beulah, the pastoral repose of Plate 1, and ends in the apocalyptic state of Eden (in Blake's sense of the term) of Plate 21. The contrasts are obvious and have often been noted: the musical instruments have been taken down from the trees in the later plate, suggesting, by way of Psalm 137, that even the original state still had something of alienation and exile about it; the sheep have wakened up, and, in contrast to the first plate, the sun is rising and the moon setting. The sacrificial altar common to the foreground of both plates contains significant inscriptions about the importance of outgrowing the literal and ritual aspects of religion which sacrifice represents. The genuine form of sacrifice, self-sacrifice, or what Blake calls the annihilation of the Selfhood, is the real subject of Plate 18.

Job is one of the "wisdom" books, and the primitive conception of wisdom, still clearly visible in the Old Testament, is that of following the tried and tested ways, the ways sanctioned by custom and tradition. This means that wisdom is primarily an attribute of advanced age, when one has had most experience in being conservative. In the Book of Proverbs and elsewhere there is a strong emphasis on bringing up young people in the ways of their seniors, and on being prompt to punish them if they diverge. There are three stages of a conflict of age and youth in the Job plates: the relation of the God of the opening plates to an obviously much younger Satan; the relation of the three friends to the youthful Elihu; and the relation of the God of the closing plates (Jehovah, more or less) to Jesus.

The God of Plates 2 and 5 is the weak, sick *dieu fainéant* who is the God projected by Job himself into the natural order. As long as a virtuous moral life can be associated with a comfortable physical one, such a deity may seem providential and benignant. But when the crunch comes he turns into Satan, the author of evil and disaster. This fact is not realized by Job, his three friends, or Elihu, all of whom try to work out some explanation of Job's plight in terms of God alone. But for Blake the God of the opening plates resigns his power to Satan in the same way that God the Father transfers power to his Son in *Paradise Lost,* and similarly demonstrates by doing so the essential link between their natures. Many years earlier Blake had remarked that "in the Book of Job, Milton's Messiah is call'd Satan."

The identity of the God of Plate 2 with Satan is clear in the nightmare of Plate 11, where at the bottom of the plate Paul's description of the Antichrist is quoted. The Antichrist is notable for his superficial resemblance to Christ, and similarly, all gods portrayed as old men in the sky are variants of the Satan whom Paul, again, calls the prince of the power of the air. Over the head of God in Plate 2 is the inscription *Malak Yahweh,* along with the translation "The Angel of the Divine Presence." This recalls the passage in *A Vision of the Last*

Judgment in which Blake speaks of "That Angel of the Divine presence mention'd in Exodus, xiv c., 19 v. & in other places; this Angel is frequently call'd by the Name of Jehovah Elohim, The 'I am' of the Oaks of Albion." Apparently Blake means that the existential reality or "I am" of God is identical with the human imagination, but when it gets projected into the outer world of nature it is perverted into something evil. Laocoon, strangled by the serpents of reasoning, is also identified by Blake with the perverted form of this Angel. In Plate 2 the primary biblical reference may be to Numbers 22:22, where the *Malak Yahweh* blocks the path of Balaam as his "Satan," or adversary. The verse in Exodus that Blake refers to reads: "And the angel of God, which went before the camp of Israel, removed and went behind them; and the pillar of the cloud went from before their face, and stood behind them." The two tendencies in man to be "idolatrous to his own shadow" and yet continually to recover his own creative powers alternate like the pillar of cloud and the pillar of fire in the Exodus story. When the Angel comes the other way, from the outer world into the human consciousness, it makes possible, for Israel, the great revolutionary feat of escaping from Egypt and achieving its own identity.

The design on Plate 5 takes the form of a vortex or gyre in which an imaginary God turns into a real devil, the order of nature which everything genuine and creative in human life has to fight against. The fall of Job repeats the fall of Adam, and its cause is the same: the pseudo-knowledge of good and evil which first tries to separate them, and ends by realizing that in such knowledge evil is the rule and good an accidental and precarious exception. This vortex is again reversed in Plate 13, where it becomes the "whirlwind" out of which God answers Job. We remember the vortex in *Milton* which takes Milton from "Heaven" to earth, earth being the place where "Heaven" has to be realized. Milton enters Blake's left foot, but ordinarily, when the projected God reverses his movement and becomes the real one, the Word of human imagination, what he enters is the ear, which is also a kind of vortex, called "labyrinthine" in *Jerusalem,* and described in *The Book of Thel,* in a very different context, as a "whirlwind fierce to draw creations in." But the God of the whirlwind in Plate 13 has to be clarified a good deal before he becomes the genuine human imagination: this process is completed in Plate 17 with the significant caption from Job 42:5: "I have heard of thee by the hearing of the ear; but now mine eye seeth thee." The only New Testament reference to Job, "Ye

have heard of the patience of Job, and have seen the end of the Lord"
(James 5:11), quoted by Blake on Plate 7, repeats this progress from
ear to eye. For Blake, no one can "see" God until God becomes a
human being, and even then he is not so much what we see as what we
see with. Some Renaissance mythographers saw in the story of Narcissus, who exchanged his identity for that of his objective reflection in
water, a counterpart to the biblical story of the fall of Adam, and
Blake, describing the fall of Albion in *Jerusalem* in imagery closely
related to the Book of Job, also speaks of Albion as becoming "idolatrous to his own shadow." The recovery by Job of his own imagination is Narcissus coming in the opposite direction, the reflected shadow
becoming his own substance.

The fact that Blake saw in the story of Job a microcosm of the
entire biblical story is the reason for the two major changes that he
makes from what is in the text: the role of Job's wife and the character
of the three friends. In the text Job's wife is a Dalila figure, a temptress
who suggests that Job renounce his integrity, and this is how Blake
depicted her in earlier illustrations of the book. In *Jerusalem* Albion's
wife, "Brittannia," is a very shadowy, not to say unnecessary, character: the main theme is the restoration to Albion of his daughter Jerusalem. This emphasis on the restored daughter (apart from the link with
King Lear, whose three daughters are also Albion's) was derived from a
parallel emphasis in the Book of Job, as illustrated here in Plate 20. But
still, when the Book of Job is thought of as a miniature Bible, Job
occupies the place of Adam or Israel or, again, Albion, the symbolic
figure of humanity, and Job's wife thus becomes the Eve or Rachel
who must form a part of his redemption.

Similarly, the three friends are almost wholly demonic in Blake's
illustrations, and are assimilated to the threefold accuser figure who
runs through all Blake's work from the early "Accusers of Theft,
Adultery and Murder" to Hand in *Jerusalem,* and who are, or is,
identified with the three accusers of Socrates (*Jerusalem* 93) and, probably, the three witnesses against Faithful in *The Pilgrim's Progress.* The
three friends have been constantly ridiculed, from the Book of Job
itself on, as "miserable comforters," and yet it is said of them, in a
verse quoted on Plate 8, that "they sat down with him upon the
ground seven days and seven nights, and none spake a word unto him:
for they saw that his grief was very great" (2:13). Seven days of silent
sympathy from friends who are at least not fair-weather friends, and
have nothing to gain from visiting Job in his destitution, may deserve

some sympathy in its turn. But when we think of Job as continuously martyred humanity, it is hardly possible to see in the friends anything but representatives of the continuous social anxiety, the Theotormon complex, so to speak, that makes human misery constant by trying to rationalize and explain it away in every crisis. We may note that a still later treatment of the Job story, MacLeish's *J.B.*, follows Blake both in favoring the wife and in denigrating the friends.

The friends, in any case, try to remain loyal to the *dieu fainéant* of the opening plates, the God of natural religion. Nature for Blake is the state of experience, indifferent to human values, exhibiting no sense of design or purpose beyond an automatic and mechanical one, and caring nothing for the individual. Job suffers not because of anything he has done but because he is in the world of Satan or Nature, like the rest of us. Satan achieved his power through God's "permission," or, to come closer to Blake, through the inevitable collapse of all efforts to unite the vision of innocence, of the world as created and protected, with the contrary vision of experience. Such efforts, we said, look plausible only to those who happen to be both "good" and prosperous. But the prosperity is a matter of luck, and Job's sufferings illustrate a principle often referred to elsewhere in Blake, that if we stay in Beulah it will sooner or later turn into "Ulro," that is, "meer Nature or hell," as Blake calls it in his notes to Swedenborg. The God of Plates 1 to 5 sooner or later turns into what Blake calls the ghost of the priest and king, the conception that rationalizes tyranny.

And just as the senile God of Plate 5 is pushed out of the way by a viciously destructive and younger Satan, so the harangues of the three friends give place to the monologue of the young Elihu, who begins with a perfunctory apology for withholding his wisdom for so long while the old men drivelled. Elihu consolidates the confused and variable notions of natural religion that the three friends propound into a closed system of fatalism. He is shown in Plate 12 pointing upwards with his left or sinister hand to a sky with twelve stars in it, representing the cycle of the Zodiac. Like all his kind, he insists on the grandeur of nature and the littleness of mankind: "Look upon the heavens and behold the clouds which are higher than thou" (cf. Job 35:5). If we have been reading the Book of Job along with Blake, we have already been told that wisdom is not there, or anywhere else in nature: "The depth saith [Wisdom] is not in me: and the sea saith, It is not with me" (28:14). Elihu has thus much the same role as that of Newton in *Europe:* he is a spokesman of natural religion so fully articulate that he overreaches himself and blows his whole system, in more than one sense, sky-high. He is a negative agent of Job's emancipation, as Newton is for Blake's time. The words in Plate 12 just quoted are attached to the figure of a sleeping old man at the bottom of creation, whose dreams rise up from his head into the stars. This figure is Blake's Albion, and the design recurs in the account of Albion's fall in *Jerusalem* 19.

The third and decisive conflict of age and youth forms the resolution of the sequence, when God as a projected old man in the sky turns into Christ, God as Man, God as the essence of Job himself, whom Job has stopped projecting into creation and has recovered as his own real nature. In Blake's mythology there are seven "Eyes," seven historical and social visions or conceptions of God, the sixth and seventh being Jehovah and Jesus. The third, Elohim, is associated with the creation of Adam, or the human form as we know it; the fourth, Shaddai, is a frequent name of God in the Book of Job. Blake may have thought the Book of Job to be or to conceal a very ancient myth, perhaps older than most of the Old Testament. Reminders of this progression of seven Eyes can be seen in the angels of the title page and the shadowy figures behind the appearance of God in the whirlwind in Plate 13. But actually every stage of history has to go through the same struggle of replacing "Jehovah," the projected old man in the sky who is Zeus and Jupiter as well, with Jesus, the divine and human Logos, who is every "Eye" when imaginatively used.

The transformation of Jehovah into Jesus occupies the four plates 14, 15, 16, and 17. Job in his original prosperity is an imaginative child, but his childlike state of innocence turns into experience, and his vision of innocence, like the child's, is driven into the submerged part of his mind, where it becomes a helpless but still defiant part of his "integrity," a bound Orc. Satan's world is a world in which everybody is an object or thing, and the pressure put on Job to make him admit that he is a thing too is very powerful, but not omnipotent. Satan's world, to adapt a phrase of Kierkegaard's, *is* but does not *exist*. Job begins to exist, in this sense, when he remains defiant and calls loudly for some explanation of what has happened to him, paying no attention to the frantic expostulations of his friends and Elihu that such an attitude is blasphemous and will only make matters worse. There is a core of truth in what they say, even in the remark that they considered Job "righteous in his own eyes." The *dieu fainéant* who turned into Satan was a creation of Job's mind, and in a sense Job keeps him in business by resisting him, somewhat as Prometheus in Shelley kept Jupiter in business until he recalled his curse.

So Job's existence is at first negative, the existence of an isolated conscious being. In this position he feels that the Satanic order is not simply indifferent but actively hostile. This attitude becomes positive with God's speech, and Job, though still isolated, begins to feel not separated from everything else but identified, or, as Blake would say, outlined. The turning point comes when he realizes that the Satanic state of experience is not something inevitable or ultimately mysterious but something to be fought, and that his dethroned vision of innocence is something that he can fight it with.

If we look at the series of Old Testament books as Blake did, and as the King James Bible usually presents them, in the Septaugint order with the books of the Apocrypha omitted, we see an order which may be the result of sheer accident, but nonetheless points to a simple and profound analysis of the Old Testament as a whole. The books from Genesis to Esther are concerned with law, history and ritual; the books from Job to Malachi with prophecy, poetry and wisdom. In this order Job would occupy the place of a poetic and prophetic version of Genesis, an account of the fall of man which avoids the moralizing and the breach of contract so dear to theological lawyers, and concentrates on the limiting of imaginative range and the mutilation of the physical body. We noticed earlier that the account of the fall in *Jerusalem* echoes Job more than it does Genesis. When Albion goes in for "imputing sin and righteousness to individuals," including himself, the Zoa Luvah, representing Urizen as well as the bound Orc, takes charge of him, smites him with sore boils, and starts him on the dreary path of misery and persecution symbolized in Blake by the "Druid" symbols of serpent and tree, which we find in the stories of the fall of Adam, the fall of Israel (Numbers 21), and the Crucifixion of Christ. We can see traces of a serpent-wound tree in the background of Plate 2.

The crucial act of renewed vision is the one between Plates 14 and 15, the vision of the Creation and the vision of Behemoth and Leviathan. Plate 14 is the reappearance of the vision of innocence, the Beulah vision of Plate 1, except that it is coming the other way, out of Job's mind and not from his circumstances. There are three levels in this plate: Job and his friends are on earth; above them is a Demiurge or creator-God controlling the order of nature; and above that is the infinite human universe, in which the morning stars and the sons of God have become the same thing. It is still an imperfect vision, because, although it does distinguish the "good" world that God originally made from the bad world that man fell into later, it has not yet detached itself from the world of experience. God's rhetorical questions about the creation, his insistence that Job was not present when the world was made, have for Blake a very different meaning from a mere attempt to shout Job down with the voice of his own superego. God is really saying: "don't look into Nature to find me: I'm not there; there's nothing there but idols and demons. Don't look for a first cause: the important question is how can you get out of your situation, not how you got into it. You are not a participant in the creation: your consciousness or imagination is something wholly detached from it. And because you are not a participant in creation you can be delivered from it." The next step is to realize that Satan is the enemy of God, that his rule is not inevitable but is to be fought by God's creative power, and that this creative power is man's creative power. This takes us into Plate 15, where there are only two levels, God and Job united on top, and below them the cycle of nature dominated by Behemoth and Leviathan.

In this plate we can see that, for Blake, Satan does not disappear from the action of the Book of Job after the prologue, nor does Job really fail to learn the truth about the Satanic origin of his calamities. Satan *is* Leviathan, looked at from the right point of view as the body of fallen nature, and not a mysterious cause of human suffering but a symptom of it to be attacked. If we had seen Job restored to prosperity, with all his brand new daughters and livestock, we might not have seen any daughter or livestock: we might have seen nothing but a beggar on a dunghill. But the beggar would know something we do not know, and would have seen something that we have not seen, which is how Leviathan looks from the outside. Leviathan being Satan revealed instead of Satan mysterious and disguised as God, he represents not only the natural miseries of drought and famine and pestilence and boils, but also the social and political miseries symbolized in the Bible by Egypt and Babylon, and in the Book of Job itself by the Sabean raiders. Ezekiel (29) identifies the Leviathan with the Pharaoh of Egypt, and Daniel (4) tells how Nebuchadnezzar of Babylon turned into a variety of Behemoth, this latter being a favorite pictorial subject for Blake. The political aspect of the two monsters is brought out in the phrases in the text emphasized by Blake on Plate 15: Behemoth is "chief of the ways of God" and Leviathan is "King over all the

Children of Pride." Their "natural" kernels are the hippopotamus and the crocodile, both Egyptian animals.

At the same time the root of human tyranny, for Blake, is still natural religion, taking the order of nature to be the circumference or horizon of all human effort, the word horizon being reflected in the name "Urizen." All of us are born inside the belly of Leviathan, the world of stars and its indefinite space, which is symbolically subterranean, the tomb out of which the Resurrection takes us, and submarine as well, for Leviathan is a sea-monster and Noah's flood has never receded. Those delivered from Leviathan, like Job and Jonah, normally have to be fished for, hence the prominence of fishing imagery in the Gospels. Similarly in Blake the kingdom of the imagination is Atlantis, underneath the "Sea of Time and Space." After Job has attained the enlightenment of Plate 15, the prophecy of Jesus is fulfilled and Satan falls from heaven in Plate 16, cast out of and separated from the divine nature. The deity in Plate 17 is unmistakably Jesus, as the New Testament quotations at the bottom of the plate make clear: if he looks older, it is because he is the divine essence of Job's own mind, and Job is an old man in Blake, if not necessarily so in the Book of Job itself. The casting out of Satan from God's nature in Plate 16 is repeated in reverse in the sacrifice scene of Plate 18, which is, as said, really a scene of self-sacrifice, and represents Job's casting the demonic principle out of himself.

Job has to be an individual, for Satan's assault on him is part of a struggle between alienation and identity, in which the former carries its conquests up to the very last stronghold of the latter, which is the individual consciousness. Everything Job *has* disappears into the illusory Satanic world of time. He is alienated from his own body by his boils, and from society by the accusing or "Elect" friends, to use the language of Blake's *Milton,* leaving Job himself in the position of the "Reprobate" prophet, the scapegoat driven like Elijah into the wilderness, with only his wife to represent "Redeemed" society. Finally Elihu, pointing to the stars so far above him, alienates him from his earlier view of God, who is now wholly replaced by the accuser. Part of the situation Job is in is one that frequently occurs in tragedy: what are the limits of one's "property," in the Aristotelian sense? That is, how much can a man lose of what he has without losing something of what he is? The implication in God's injunction to Satan, that he could take away whatever Job had but not his life, is that Job's identity must remain untouched: the test is whether he will cling to that identity or throw it away. As he is not being punished for anything but tested, the metaphor of a "trial" or lawsuit, held in a court of God with accusers and defendants, hangs over the entire book. Job keeps trying to identify his prosecutor and to call on his advocate (the word translated "redeemer" in 19:25), and he eventually finds that his accuser is the ghost or "Spectre" of his redeemer.

But a trial is a social metaphor, and Job has to represent, not simply an individual, but mankind as a whole. If we think of God as a trinity of power and wisdom and love, it may seem strange that there is so much about God's power and wisdom in the Book of Job and so little about love of any kind. But the implications of the social dimension of love are there in the text, and Blake makes them the main subject of the final three plates. We are told, in a passage quoted on Plate 18, that Job's captivity was "turned" when he prayed for his friends; the friends are received into the new community in Plate 19, and the family, symbolized by the three daughters, is reestablished in Plate 20. In Plate 1 we see a community of twelve, Job, his wife, his seven sons, and his three daughters, making up a figure of the twelve-fold Israel who, in Blake's view of the Exodus, achieved liberation from Egypt only to be enslaved once again by the hypnotizing twelve-fold Zodiac of stars over their heads:

> That fiery joy, that Urizen perverted to ten commands,
> What time he led the starry host through the wide
>   wilderness.
>
> (America, Plate 8)

In Plate 21 this community of twelve is restored, with the differences from the beginning already noted.

The ambiguity between Job as individual and Job as social being or patriarch is of a kind central to all mythical structures of this descent-and-return shape. The suffering Job must be an individual, but when we think of the restored Job as an individual too, continuous with his previous sufferings, difficulties arise. The origin of the Book of Job appears to have been an ancient folktale preserved in the prose opening and ending of the book we now have, and in such a folktale the restoration of Job as an individual can be accepted without question. But for the book we have, restoration of an individual alone could only be an arbitrary act of a deity separate from Job, and a somewhat vulgar act at that, because of its elimination of love. Even in a society as patriarchal as Job's, three new daughters would hardly "make up for" the loss of the previous daughters. We can see the restoring of an individual Job, perhaps, in terms of the analogy of waking up from a dream, where anxiety and humiliation are dealt with simply by abolishing the world in which they exist. But if the restoration of Job is not imaginatively continuous with his misery, what is the point of the poem? If, when Job improves his state of mind or his theology, his misery disappears too, we go back to the point at which the book began, and, in spite of the phrase "twice as much as he had before" (42:10), the book itself becomes meaningless. To say that Job is restored in a different world from the world of his sufferings would be more logically consistent, but it would considerably impoverish the human significance of the story.

The general critical principle involved is that in a descent-and-return mythical structure, as a rule, only the individual descends; only the community returns. Temptation, alienation, despair, decisive choice, death itself, are ordeals that only the individual can carry to their limit. But only a re-created society, like the one that crystallizes in the final scene of a comedy around a hero's marriage, can fully experience the sense of redemption. In Plate 20 Job's arms, outspread over his daughters, show that he with his daughters forms part of a larger human body, so that although the objective order from which his calamities came has been annihilated for Job (the calamities being depicted on the walls "In the shadows of Possibility," as Blake says in *Jerusalem*), Job's renewed state is not a subjective one. His daughters constitute his "Emanation," the total body of what he loves and creates through love. The ambiguity of the phrase "human body," which may be an individual or a social body, is involved in the contrast between the natural body which dies and the spiritual body which rises again. Job has what Paul calls a "vile body," given over to boils, but it is in his "flesh" (19:26) that he sees the God who appears in Plate 17.

At the beginning of the creation we are told that "the earth was without form, and void; and darkness was upon the face of the deep." Darkness and chaos, the latter being symbolized by the sea, have a twofold role in the Bible. They are, essentially, Satan and the Leviathan, and hence Satan and the Leviathan may be thought of as eternally enemies of God, totally shut out of the divine nature, reduced to annihilation at the Last Judgement. (In traditional Christianity they go on surviving indefinitely in hell, along with most of the human race, but that doctrine was for Blake a political ploy on the part of the

Church, and a most contemptible one.) Yet, we are also told, the first act of creation was to separate light from darkness, and the second to separate land from sea. Hence darkness and chaos are also dialectically incorporated into the creation, and therefore Satan and the Leviathan could also, in a different context, be regarded as creatures of God, on whom God would look with a by no means unfriendly eye. They are so regarded in the Book of Job, though nowhere else in the Bible.

The question of whether death was also incorporated into the original creation is more difficult. For man, according to Genesis, death came only as a consequence of disobedience. In any case we are now confronted by a nature with death as well as darkness and chaos built into it, and have to realize the influence on our minds of two gods. One, who allowed darkness, chaos and death into the natural order, is really Satan, the death-impulse in us, and the other is Jesus, who escaped from death and is our own essential life. Blake's Laocoön engraving describes the three figures of the sculpture as Jehovah with his two sons Satan and Adam, and around "Jehovah's" head he puts, in addition to the "*Malak Yahweh*" and "Angel of the Divine Presence" already mentioned, the inscription:

> He repented that he had made Adam (of the Female, the Adamah) & it grieved him at his heart.

This last phrase, from Genesis 6:6, is also quoted in the Job illustrations (Plate 5), and the rest of it is from the Hebrew text of Genesis 2:7. The total meaning is that the alleged creation of Adam was really the separating of a subjective consciousness from an objective existence, a dying mind from a dead body. The "lapsed Soul" of the "Introduction" to the *Songs of Experience* is not Adam, but the unity of man (*adam*) with the nature and the rest of life (the female *adamah* or "ground"), which are now united only by death.

The traditional creating God, then, is really a destroying God, the flood being another version of the creation of the order of nature at the beginning of the Bible, including man as he now exists. This "creation" is at the opposite pole from the destruction of the world by fire prophesied in the Book of Revelation at the end. Such a destruction would be an utterly pointless firework display if we did not realize that the traditional creation was itself a destruction, and the traditional destruction in the future the real creation and the manifesting again of what was there before the so-called creation. The Book of Job, for Blake, tells the same story of his own *Jerusalem,* whose theme is:

> Of the Sleep of Ulro! and of the passage through
> Eternal Death! and of the awaking to Eternal Life.

But it also tells the story of the "Bible of Hell," the Bible as Blake read it. The God who saves man is not a God who comes down out of the sky to impose order and authority and obedience, but a God who bursts out of the tomb of death with his face blackened by the soot of hell. This is the drama going on behind the wings of the quiet sequence of visions in the last third of the Job engravings. Blake's vision of the Book of Job was certainly a work of the creative imagination, but what made it possible was a powerful critical analysis of the book, of the whole Bible of which it forms a microcosm, and of the human life which, according to Matthew Arnold, is the theatre in which creation and criticism have become the same thing.

God under Attack

David Daiches

The only completed successful epic poem in the English language is Milton's *Paradise Lost*. It differs from all the other great epics of the Western world by having a precise theological aim: to justify the ways of God to men. Milton is here using the word "justify" in the third definition of the word given in the *Oxford English Dictionary*: "to show . . . to be just or in the right." That God, who is by definition just and right as well as omnipotent, should require justification by a human poet seems somewhat extraordinary. To justify the ways of men to God might seem a reasonable undertaking, but to justify the ways of God to men implies that there is prima facie evidence that God deals unjustly with men and that God is in need of a defence. Further, Milton sees that defence as especially needed by religious people, by committed Christians indeed, that "fit audience though few" to whom his poem is addressed. It seems therefore that he considered the account of God's dealings with men as revealed in the Old and New Testaments to be in itself an inadequate explanation of the inconsistencies between the concept of an all-good and all-powerful God and the facts of human experience. Milton went further than that. In his posthumously published Latin work on Christian doctrine he stated boldly that the facts of human experience "have compelled all nations to believe, either that God, or that some evil power whose name was unknown, presided over the affairs of the world." He considered the

From *God and the Poets: The Gifford Lectures, 1983*. © 1984 by David Daiches. Clarendon Press, 1984.

view that evil ruled the world to be "as unmeet as it is incredible," yet he conceded that it was warranted by simple observation of what happens to men in the world.

The dilemma is of course an ancient one: how to reconcile human suffering, especially the suffering of the righteous, with the existence of an omnipotent God of justice and love. This question of theodicy, the vindication of God's justice, is quite separate from the question of God's existence, which Milton took for granted just as the authors of the Bible took it for granted. In the Psalms there is never any question of God's existence, apart from the remark at the beginning of Psalm 53: "The fool hath said in his heart, there is no God." There is no argument; the atheist is simply a fool. (The Hebrew word used here, *naval,* can really mean either.) But there is much anguish over God's dealings with men, over the sufferings of the virtuous and the prosperity of the wicked. While many of the Psalms assure us that the righteous shall prosper and the wicked shall be destroyed—the very first Psalm is an eloquent statement of this position—there are as many that ask the question put most directly in Psalm 94: "Lord, how long shall the wicked triumph?" There is the cry for help in Psalm 12: "Help, Lord; for the godly man ceaseth; for the faithful fail among the children of men." There is the bitter question of Psalm 22: "My God, my God, why hast thou forsaken me?" Every kind of variation is played on the theme of the good man left to misery and suffering and the wicked man prospering. "The wicked walk on every side, when the vilest men are exalted" is the desperate conclusion of Psalm 12. Side by side with these protests we find great outbursts of confidence that the Lord will in the end reward the good and punish the bad, most strongly of all in Psalm 37, which goes so far as to make a statement, said to derive from experience but which in fact seems to run counter to what we experience in the real world: "I have been young, and now am old; yet have I not seen the righteous forsaken, nor his seed begging bread." If Milton could have accepted this, he would not have felt the need to write *Paradise Lost.*

Milton's justification of God was, at least on the surface, based on his explanation of the fact that God endowed the first man with free will and that punishment of him and his descendants for the abuse of that free will was perfectly just, while the Christian scheme of redemption, that allowed a tiny minority of the world's inhabitants throughout history to gain salvation through acceptance of Christ's sacrifice, was a mitigation of strict justice by love. What Milton really made of this argument in *Paradise Lost* is a topic I wish to return to [elsewhere]. At this stage I am concerned with the general problem of theodicy as it impinged on poets who accepted without question the existence of an omnipotent God. The Psalms mingle praise of God, anguished questioning of his justice, and confidence that all will be well in the end. The praise and the confidence represented what might be called the orthodox position. The implications of this position could be disturbing. If God did really punish the wicked and reward the virtuous, then it would seem that misfortune was evidence of prior wickedness, and happiness and prosperity a sign of virtue. The Mosaic injunctions as formulated in chapter 28 of Deuteronomy make it clear that obedience to God's law will bring happiness and prosperity and disobedience will bring misfortune and suffering. The Hebrew prophets saw the sufferings of their people, especially their conquest and exile, as punishment for wrongdoing. Now it is one thing to say that society as a whole will suffer in the long run if its members persistently practise injustice, but it is quite another to see individual, personal fortune as the direct consequence of the individual's degree of virtue, so that the virtuous prosper and the wicked do not. As I have noted, experience contradicts this and has been acknowledged to contradict this from ancient times. This has not prevented religious leaders from proclaiming this doctrine. It was precisely because they did so that people were lead to reflect on the relation between doctrine and experience and the problems of theodicy that they raised. It was the poets who first raised the question, which was simply this: We do not dispute God's existence or his power; but what about his justice? This was the question posed by the greatest of all the poets of theodicy, the author of that remarkable dramatic poem we call the Book of Job.

The Book of Job uses an old folktale for its beginning and its ending. The folktale is of a good and prosperous man who was tried by every kind of misfortune and affliction but who in spite of everything bore all misfortunes patiently and without losing faith in God until he was rewarded by a restoration of all he had lost and increased happiness and prosperity. The first and last chapters of the existing Book of Job tell this story, and there is evidence that they are considerably older than the main part of the book, not only from the style and language, which belong to simple folk-history, but also from the phrase "the patience of Job," which antedates the book as we have it and refers to the simple tale of trust and patience rewarded. Between the opening and closing brackets, that derive from the old folktale, a great poet has inserted a dramatic poem of extraordinary richness and vitality, powerful in imagery, often difficult in language, bold in thought, that confronts the question of the justice of God's dealings with men. Job here is not the patient Job of the folktale. Far from it: he is angry to the point of blasphemy and keeps demanding an explanation from God.

The opening chapter introduces us to Job as a virtuous, God-fearing man who is also rich and highly esteemed. He is not an Israelite, but located in the land of Uz, which cannot be definitely identified. The scene changes to God reviewing his angels, among whom is the Satan (note the definite article: Satan is not yet a proper name, nor does it refer to the Devil: the Satan was an angel, the accuser, the prosecuting counsel among the angels whose task was to find out and report on evil acts in the world). God boasts about the exemplary virtue of his servant Job, and the Satan replies that it is easy to be virtuous when everything goes well: change his good fortune to misery and see what happens. God gives the Satan permission to do this. Job loses all his possessions and his children, but he does not lose his trust in God. Then, at a further assembly in Heaven, the Satan points out that Job has not been afflicted in his physical person, and God gives him permission to afflict Job in this way, so long as his life is spared. So Job is afflicted with sore boils and is both unsightly and in agony. This virtuous man has now lost all his possessions, his children, and his physical well-being: he is disgusting to look at. His impatient wife tells him to curse God and die, but Job replies: "Shall we receive good at the hand of God and not receive evil?" and repudiates the advice. He sits on an ashpit outside his house and mourns in silence. Three friends then come to visit him, and respect his grief by waiting in silence for seven days and nights. At the end of that period Job begins to speak. And with the lyric lamentation that bursts from his lips we enter into the real, poetical Book of Job.

The compact energy of Job's lyric cry is difficult to render in English. According to the Authorized Version, the lament begins:

Let the day perish wherein I was born
And the night in which it was said, There is a man child
    conceived.

That is twenty-two words to eight of the original Hebrew, which moreover contains a pun, on the words יֹאבַד ("let it perish") and

אוּלַד ("I was born"). Something of the forceful brevity of the original is suggested by Marvin Pope's rendering [in *The Anchor Bible: Job*]:

> Damn the day I was born,
> The night that said, "A boy is begot."

He regrets having been born, and wishes that at least he had died at birth. In the grave there is release from suffering (Job knows nothing of an afterlife) and true equality: there kings and princes lie at rest with their humble subjects.

> There the wicked cease from troubling,
> And there the weary are at rest.

At this stage Job is not arguing; he is lamenting. He yearns for death, which comes not, and seeks after it more than for hidden treasure. His way is hidden: God has fenced him in. The lament ends with a sentence that is not adequately rendered by the King James translators:

$$\text{לֹא שָׁלַוְתִּי וְלֹא שָׁקַטְתִּי}$$

$$\text{וְלֹא־נַחְתִּי וַיָּבֹא רֹגֶז׃}$$

Eight powerful and incisive Hebrew words, which can perhaps be rendered:

> I have no rest, no peace;
> What has come is agony.

Job is not yet directly arraigning God's justice: he is expressing his total disillusion with life and his wish for death. His complaint is answered by Eliphaz, the first of the three friends. Like his two colleagues, he speaks for the orthodox view that God punishes the wicked and rewards the virtuous here on earth. At first he tries to reassure Job that if he is really virtuous, things are bound to turn out all right for him:

> Is not your fear of God your confidence,
> Your hope your upright conduct?

> Remember, pray, whoever perished being innocent,
> Or where were the upright cut off?

Well, Job was innocent and upright, and he has, in a sense, "perished" and been "cut off." Eliphaz seems to realize that this *argumentum ad hominem* won't work, so he turns to generalities before introducing a new note. In the sight of God, *nobody,* not even the angels, can be truly virtuous. This thought is expressed as a strange, visionary insight, that came to him in the dead of night, when a spirit seemed to pass before him, so that his bones shook and his hair stood on end, and a voice proclaimed

> Shall mortal man be more just than God?
> Shall a man be more pure than his maker?
>
> Behold, he put no trust in his servants:
> And his angels he charged with folly.
>
> How much more them that dwell in houses of clay,
> Whose foundation is in the dust,
> Who are crushed before the moth.

The frisson that accompanies this vision and this mystical utterance cannot alter the fact that it does not help Job. If all the creatures created by God are imperfect in his sight, that might well be a reflection on God's handiwork. The point is, by what guilt of their own did they become imperfect? (Milton faces, albeit briefly, the question of hereditary guilt, when he has Adam admit that his progeny will be justly held guilty because of his offence, but such a thought is far from the author of the Book of Job.) Eliphaz does not himself seem to be sure of the implications of his vision for Job's case, for he leaves this point abruptly and goes on to cite a number of proverbial sayings about God frustrating the wicked and saving the virtuous poor from the hand of the mighty. Again, this does not seem to be relevant to Job's case. He then moves on to a quite new point, which would be relevant to Job's case if Job accepted it.

> Behold, happy is the man whom God correcteth;
> Therefore despise not the chastening of the Almighty.

The implications of this are not pursued, however, and Eliphaz goes on to cite in traditional form cases of the goodness and care of God. Here the rendering in the Authorized Version conveys the feel of the original very well:

> He shall deliver thee in six troubles,
> Yea in seven shall no evil touch thee.

> In famine he shall redeem thee from death,
> And in war from the power of the sword. . . .

> At destruction and famine thou shalt laugh,
> Neither shalt thou be afraid of the beasts of the earth. . . .

> Thou shalt know also that thy seed shall be great,
> And thy offspring as the grass of the earth.

> Thou shalt come to thy grave in a full age,
> Like as a shock of corn cometh in in his season.

"You are going to be all right, Job" is what these concluding sentences of Eliphaz's speech amount to. But Job is in no mood to be comforted by traditional proverbs. In his reply he ignores Eliphaz's arguments and continues his lament. He says that God has grievously persecuted him and again says that he wishes for death. As for his friend's words, they are like the wadis of Syria and Palestine, rushing torrents in the rainy season but dry and desolate in the summer when the traveller needs them. Nothing that has been said is of any help to him in his misery. He pleads with God to remember that his life is but a breath and that it is time God let him go. Only in death will he escape from God's watchful persecution. Here Job embarks on a daring parody of the Psalmist's view of God's watchful care for man. He is not directly arraigning God.

> Am I a sea, or a sea-monster,
> That thou settest a watch over me?

In Psalm 8 the author takes pride and comfort in the fact that God is mindful of man:

> When I consider thy heavens, the work of thy fingers,
> The moon and the stars which thou hast ordained,

> What is man, that thou art mindful of him?
> And the son of man that thou visitest him?

> For thou hast made him a little lower than the angels,
> And hast crowned him with glory and honour.

This is directly parodied by Job:

> What is man, that thou shouldst magnify him,
> And that thou shouldst set thy heart upon him?

> And that thou shouldst visit him every morning,
> And try him every moment?

> Will you never look away from me,
> Nor let me alone till I swallow down my spittle?

This is being hounded by a Hound of Heaven indeed.

Even if he has sinned, Job goes on—and it is made clear later that if he has, God has not told him what he is charged with—how can that affect God: "What difference does it make to you, man watcher?" That terrible phrase נֹצֵר הָאָדָם, "man watcher," spat out in fury, completes the reversal of the Psalmist's view.

This second speech of Job modulates at its conclusion into a minor key. If he has committed some sin of which he is unaware, why will not God forgive him and let him die in peace? That last line, וְשִׁחַרְתַּנִי וְאֵינֶנִּי, —"you would look for me then and I wouldn't be there"—has a curious note of self-pity, as though he is saying, "You'll be sorry then, God." It always reminds me of that passage in Joyce's *Portrait of the Artist as a Young Man* when the young Stephen, lying sick in the school sick-bay, contemplates his own death and funeral and thinks how sorry the school bully will be *then*.

The second of the three visitors, Bildad, then answers Job. He begins with less courtesy than Eliphaz had shown, being clearly shocked by Job's attitude as revealed in his second speech. But all he has to say is to repeat the traditional view that God punishes sinners and rewards the virtuous. He has not the slightest doubt that a simple law of retribution prevails. If you were pure and upright, he tells Job, you would not be suffering now. For that, he says, is the view of all former generations. Can we know better than our ancestors? With considerable poetic liveliness he plays variations on the theme of God's retributive justice, concluding with words reminiscent of one of the moods of the Psalms:

> Behold, God will not cast away a perfect man,
> Neither will he help the evil-doers;

> Till he fill thy mouth with laughing,
> And thy lips with rejoicing.

> They that hate thee shall be clothed with shame,
> And the dwelling-place of the wicked shall come to nought.

Bildad has not yet reached the position where he says that Job must have been an evil-doer or he would not be suffering as he is—that is to come later. True, he begins by saying that if he had been virtuous he would not be suffering now, but he seems to backtrack in his conclusion, when he reassures Job that if he has been virtuous all will eventually be well with him. He does not quite see which horn of the dilemma to come to rest on.

In his reply Job totally ignores Bildad's arguments. His object is to draw up an indictment of the way God administers human affairs. He does not need to be persuaded of God's power, of which Eliphaz had painted a vivid picture. He can describe that as eloquently as anyone:

> Who removeth the mountains and they know it not,
> Who overturneth them in his anger.
>
> Who shaketh the earth out of her place,
> And the pillars thereof tremble.
>
> Who commandeth the sun, and it riseth not,
> And sealeth up the stars.
>
> Who alone spreadeth out the heavens,
> And treadeth upon the waves of the sea.
>
> Who maketh the Bear, Orion and the Pleiades,
> And the chambers of the south.
>
> Who doeth great things past finding out,
> Yea, marvellous things without number.

He is a powerful God, and also a hidden God, a *deus absconditus;* אֵל מִסְתַּתֵּר as the Deutero-Isaiah called him:

> Lo, he goeth by me, and I see him not;
> He passeth on also, but I perceive him not.

No one can call God to account.

> Who will say unto him: "What doest thou?"

How can he argue before God, who could break him with a tempest and would not suffer him to take his breath? Then come the crux of Job's case:

> If it is a matter of strength, yes, he is mighty.
> But if it is a matter of justice, who could arraign him?

אִם לְכֹחַ אַמִּיץ הִנֵּה

וְאִם לְמִשְׁפָּט מִי יוֹעִידֵנוּ

(Accepting Pope's emendation of יוֹעִידֵנִי to יוֹעִידֵנוּ) God, supreme in power, is subject to no court; no one can make a legal plea before him. Further, God can force the innocent to confess guilt:

> Even though I be righteous, mine own mouth shall condemn
> me;
> Though I be innocent, he shall prove me perverse.

> I am innocent: I care not for myself;
> I despise my life.

> It is all one: therefore I say,
> He destroys the innocent and the wicked.

> If the scourge slay suddenly,
> He will laugh at the calamity of the innocent.

> The earth is given into the hand of the wicked;
> He covereth the faces of the judges thereof.
> If not he—then who?

אִם־לֹא אֵפוֹ מִי־הוּא.

God is responsible. Job does not take a Manichaean position, but accepts the traditional view that God is the creator of *everything,* including evil. The Deutero-Isaiah had made this point quite explicitly:

> I form the light, and create darkness.
> I make peace, and create evil.
> I the Lord do all these things.

It is not Satan, the Prince of Darkness, who creates evil. God is all-powerful and is the creator of everything that exists. But Isaiah did not draw Job's conclusion, which is that if God did it all, he is responsible, he is to blame.

Job now goes further. One cannot get justice from God because there is no one above him to act as arbitrator between him and his suffering creature. I am found guilty already, he says: "why then do I labour in vain?" He makes the point quite precisely in an incisive sentence לֹא יֵשׁ בֵּינֵינוּ מוֹכִיח there is between us no *mochiah,* no um-pire, who can listen impartially to both points of view. The urgency and the passion rise as Job now pleads with God to let him approach him and plead his cause.

> Let him take his rod away from me
> And let not his fear terrify me:
> Then would I speak and not fear him.

Let God stop exercising power and exercise justice. Let him at least tell Job what the case against him is. "Make me know wherefore thou contendest with me." He goes on to ask God if he knows what it is like to be a man.

> Hast thou eyes of flesh,
> Or seest thou as man seeth?
>
> Are thy days as the days of man,
> Are thy years as man's days,
>
> That thou inquirest after mine iniquity
> And searchest after my sin,
>
> Although thou knowest that I am not guilty
> And there is no escape out of thy hand?

After all, he goes on in a moving passage expressing the mystery of conception and uterine growth, it was God who made him:

> Remember, I beseech thee, that thou hast made me as the clay;
> And wilt thou bring me into dust again?
>
> Hast thou not poured me out as milk,
> And curdled me like cheese?
>
> Thou hast clothed me with skin and flesh
> And knit me with bones and sinews.

Yet all the time, Job continues, God was hiding his dark intention of ultimately reducing him to misery, regardless of whether he were wicked or virtuous. What then was the use of his having been born?

> Wherefore then hast thou brought me forth out of the womb?
> Would that I had died, and no eye had seen me!
>
> I should have been as though I had not been
> And been carried from womb to grave.

> Are not my days few? Let me be,
> Turn away from me so that I may have a little comfort
>
> Before I go, never to return,
> To a land of darkness and gloom,
>
> A land of thick darkness, like darkness itself,
> Of utter gloom without order
> Where the light is as darkness.

The third visitor, Zophar, now enters the argument. He denounces Job's insistence on his guiltlessness as arrogant boasting. God knows what he is doing and can spy iniquity when men think he does not see. If Job repents of the evil he *must* have done, then all will be well with him. At this point Zophar falls into the standard poetic description of the security and hope of the virtuous and the plight of the wicked. Job's reply shows his exasperation. It begins with bitter irony:

> No doubt but ye are the people,
> And wisdom shall die with you.

He knows the truth as well as they, and the truth is that he has become a laughing-stock to his neighbours. Those who are comfortable are not concerned with the misfortunes of others.

> The tents of robbers prosper
> And they that provoke God are secure.

The very beasts of the field and birds of the air know this. They know that it is God who has done all this:

> Who knoweth not in all these
> That the hand of the Lord hath wrought this?

This again is a bitter parody of a common thought in earlier biblical literature. But it is not wonders that the hand of the Lord hath wrought so far as Job is concerned: it is injustice. God's power is in fact destructive:

> Behold he destroyeth, and it cannot be built again;
> He shutteth up a man, and there can be no opening.
>
> Behold, he withholdeth the waters, and they dry up;
> Also he sendeth them out, and they overturn the earth.

With him are strength and victory,
The deceived and the deceiver are both his.

He leadeth counsellors away stripped
And of judges he maketh fools.

Job goes on to list God's activities in loosening and binding kings, in stripping priests and taking away the reason of elders, in making nations great and then destroying them, in making imbeciles of wise men and leaders, in short of playing havoc with human order so that men grope in darkness without light and stagger like drunkards. He does not need to be told about God's activities by his friends.

Then comes a remarkable turn in Job's argument, when he makes a point he reiterates in subsequent chapters of the book:

Notwithstanding I would speak to the Almighty,
And I desire to reason with God.

This is to emerge as a central demand of Job's. He wants a chance to put his case before God. Even if God destroys him, he will persist in this demand. He is determined to put his case *against* God *to* God. He cries:

Yes, he may slay me: I have no hope:
But I will argue my case to his face!

(This is the famous passage that has been traditionally rendered: "Though he slay me, yet will I trust in him: but I will maintain mine own ways before him." The Hebrew word for "not" and the Hebrew word for "to him" sound the same but are spelled differently. The text has the word, *lo,* spelled *lamed aleph,* meaning "not," but the Masoretes, the Jewish scribes who edited and vocalized the Hebrew text of the Bible, put in the margin that though the text read *lo* meaning "not" it should be read as though it were *lo* spelled *lamed vav* meaning "to him" or "in him," thus avoiding what seemed to them a blasphemous implication. Generations of readers have as a consequence taken this sentence as a ringing declaration of faith in the midst of despair. Unfortunately, as all scholars agree, the meaning of the Hebrew *lo ayachel* is certainly "I have no hope" or something like that and cannot mean "I will trust in him." Job is saying that even though God pursues him to death, he will insist on his right to confront him and present his case.)

Job goes on to appeal to God to hear him. He has, he says, prepared his case and he knows that he would be acquitted if given a chance to present it. The language here is the language of the law-courts. It has been suggested that Job's question "Who is he that will contend with me?" is the opening formula of a plaintiff in a lawcourt. Certainly the Hebrew word translated as "contend" has the connotation of "dispute" in the legal sense, and the noun from the same root can mean both a quarrel and a lawsuit.

After the recital of this legal formula, Job appeals to God:

> Withdraw thy hand far from me,
> And let not thy terror make me afraid.
>
> Then call thou, and I will answer,
> And let me speak and answer thou me.
>
> How many are mine iniquities and sins?
> Let me know my transgression and my sin.

As he makes even clearer later, Job feels that if he is being punished for something he has done, he has the right to know what he is accused of. To be found guilty and punished before the case has even come to court and without the accused having any idea of what he is charged with is not in accordance with justice, still less so when, as in this case, the accuser, the judge, and the punisher are the same individual.

Job then breaks into an elegiac lyric:

> Man that is born of a woman
> Is of few days, and full of trouble.

Man's life passes like a shadow. (One is reminded of Pindar's description of human life as σκιᾶς ὄυρ, the dream of a shadow.) If a tree is cut down it will sprout again, but "man lieth down and riseth not." The thought strikes him that *if* there were a life after death there might be an opportunity then for a dialogue with God:

> If a man die, may he live again?
> All my weary days I would wait
> Till my relief should come.
>
> Thou wouldst call and I would answer thee
> Thou wouldst care for the work of thy hands.
>
> But as things are, thou numberest my steps,
> Thou dost not even wait for my sin.

This moving expression of a rapprochement with God after death represents a momentary hope, which soon fades. For Job there is no recompense for the sorrows of this world in the next. This speech of Job's ends with his relapsing into total pessimism, and on this note the first cycle of speeches concludes.

The second cycle begins with Eliphaz elaborating once again the traditional view. No man is perfect, therefore no man has a right to complain if suffering comes upon him. As for the sinner, even when he seems to be at peace and happy he is inwardly troubled. Eliphaz ends by giving an eloquent description of the ultimate fate of the wicked. It is interesting that in presenting the traditional morality against which the Book of Job is a protest the author puts passionate and persuasive poetry into the mouths of Job's friends. They are not made to seem feeble or stupid, any more than Milton's fallen angels are made to seem feeble or stupid when he presents them debating. This helps to give the book great dramatic power. The positions put forward by Job's friends are deeply felt and often expressed with moving conviction. But they never really meet the points that Job makes. "Sorry comforters are ye all" says Job to the three of them after Eliphaz has concluded his second speech.

After dismissing his friends' "windy words" and remarking that he could speak like that too if their positions were reversed, Job turns again to God, charging him with having betrayed and broken him even though he is innocent. He cries out:

> O earth, cover not thou my blood,
> And let my cry have no resting-place.

But then his note changes quite remarkably. He turns from God the arbitrary wielder of power to God the dispenser of justice. Surely there is somebody on high who will bear witness on his behalf:

> Even now, behold, my witness is in heaven
> And he that testifieth for me is on high.

The single word here rendered as "he that testifieth for me" is an Aramaic word, *sahed,* meaning "witness," which is also the meaning of the noun in the previous line. Marvin Pope renders it "guarantor" and comments: "Many exegetes take the heavenly witness here to be God himself, the God of justice and steadfast love, to whom Job appeals against the God of wrath. . . . In this context, however, the heavenly witness, guarantor, friend can scarcely be God who is already Accuser, Judge, and Executioner." This view seems to be borne out by the verses that immediately follow:

> Are my friends my intercessors?
> It is to God that mine eye poureth out tears,
>
> That he would set a judge between a man and God
> As a man does for his neighbour.

But the Hebrew text here has clearly suffered damage and the precise meaning cannot be certain. It seems fairly clear that although the thought starts off as meaning something like "Rather God than *these* friends, in spite of everything," it moves on to suggest the need for a judge (just as he had earlier asked for an umpire) between man and God, a third party who would arbitrate between them. Always hovering in the background, however, is the thought that the powerful God who is responsible for Job's suffering is also the God of justice and of love and there must be some way of appealing from one to the other. It is as though Job cannot reconcile himself to a view of God as simply hostile. He does not pursue this line any further at this stage, but returns to elegy:

> For the few years pass,
> And I go the way of no return.
>
> My spirit is broken, my days are spent:
> It is the grave for me.

This speech of Job's ends in total gloom:

> Where then is my hope?
> My hope, who can see it?
>
> It goes down with me to Sheol,
> Together we shall descend to the dust.

The movement to and fro between indignation and elegy, between defiance and self-pity, and more fundamentally between despair and hope, is part of the fabric of the poetry of Job's speeches. When we think of his passionate cry, "O earth cover not thou my blood," we may be reminded of the last great cry of Prometheus at the end of Aeschylus's play *Prometheus Bound*, ἐσορᾷς μ' ὡς ἔκδικα πάσχω— "You see me, how I suffer injustice." But the situation there is really very different from that in Job. Prometheus is being punished by Zeus for something that he did, and although Prometheus does not consider his action in bringing fire down to man as a crime, Zeus does, and Prometheus knows that Zeus does. Further, Zeus is shown clearly as a tyrant, and there is the suggestion in the play that the time will eventually come when he will modify his position and learn to abate his tyranny. Aeschylus's play is not an enquiry into the bases of Zeus's activity. The Book of Job *is* an enquiry into the bases of God's activity. It is an enquiry forced on Job by his own experience and is conducted not so much by an amassing of evidence as by the fluctuations of feeling.

Bildad now replies again to Job, evincing no sympathy whatever for his plight nor understanding of his arguments. He is outraged by Job's attitude, and having expressed his outrage he goes on to repeat the old argument. If Job suffers, he must have erred: the wicked always meet an appropriate fate. He describes the fate of the wicked at some length, with the implication that what has happened to Job shows him to have been wicked. Job then rounds on him and asks how long will he torment him with words. He is *not* guilty and is not being punished for wickedness. He can get no answer from God. אֲשַׁוֵּעַ וְאֵין מִשְׁפָּט —"I cry out, but there is no justice." God has destroyed him absolutely. His kinsfolk and friends have failed him, his servants have abandoned him, his wife finds him loathsome, even street urchins despise him. And those whom he loved have turned against him. In desperation he turns from crying to God to crying to his three friends.

> Have pity on me, have pity on me, O ye my friends,
> For the hand of God hath touched me.

> Why do ye persecute me like God
> And are not satisfied with my flesh?

He wishes that his words were written down and permanently graven in rock. He does not say why, but the implication is that he wishes his case to be on permanent record. But the thought turns at once into something different and surprising:

> But as for me, I know that my vindicator liveth
> And that he will at last arise upon earth.

The traditional translation here of course is the famous "I know that my Redeemer liveth," which has all sorts of theological implications read into it. But the Hebrew word גאל, *goel*, means a vindicator; it is used in Deuteronomy and 2 Samuel to denote the nearest kinsman whose duty it was to exact vengeance in a blood feud. By extension, God came later to be called "*goel Yisrael*," generally rendered Redeemer of Israel, but it seems clear that it is the original basic meaning that is intended here. The real question concerns the identity of the vindicator in whom, in an unexpected surge of confidence, Job affirms his belief. Is he saying, "I know that eventually someone will arise to defend me against the injustices from which I suffer at God's hand," or is he saying in what Robert Gordis in his edition of the book calls "a moment of mystical ecstasy" that God himself will in the end vindicate him? Scholars differ, as they differ too on the interpretation of the difficult and evidently textually corrupt passage that follows. The Authorized Version renders it

> And though after my skin worms destroy this body,
> Yet in my flesh shall I see God.

The New English Bible takes the whole passage in a legal sense and translates:

> But in my heart I know that my vindicator lives
> and that he will rise at last to speak in court;
> and I shall discern my witness standing at my side
> and see my defending counsel, even God himself.

This reading is based on emendations of a partly unintelligible text. Marvin Pope renders:

> Even after my skin is flayed
> Without my flesh I shall see God.

Robert Gordis renders:

> Deep in my skin this has been marked,
> and in my very flesh do I see God.

It is a pity that at such a critical moment in the expression of Job's changing attitudes the text is so obscure. But there seems little doubt that Job is expressing confidence in his vindication, and whether we interpret the *goel* to be God or to be some other vindicator, in the end he will have a satisfactory face-to-face resolution of the matter with God. Gordis's rendering of what he considers a transitory moment of mystical vision in the present tense ("and in my very flesh do I see God") is in conformity with his view that this is a fleeting moment of ecstasy that Job cannot sustain. One cannot be certain of this. It does however seem to be a moment of visionary confidence in the ultimate happy ending, and it is true it is not sustained.

Zophar now answers with a speech that is an impressive weaving together of thoughts found in the Psalms and elsewhere in biblical literature of the shortness of the triumph of the wicked and their eventual condign punishment. Even if the sinner is not immediately punished he will be inwardly miserable as he awaits his inevitable doom. It is a picture presented with passionate eloquence, but of course it is of no help to Job. Job's reply simply denies outright the truth of Zophar's statements. The wicked prosper; they do not suffer; look around and you will see.

> How oft is the lamp of the wicked put out?
> That their calamity cometh upon them?
> That God distributeth pains in his anger?

The wicked die unpunished, at ease and quiet. There is no correlation between what happens to a man and his degree of virtue. The good and evil in the end lie down alike in the dust and the worms get them both. His friends can ask rhetorically where one can find the flourishing houses of the wicked. Just ask any traveller, says Job: you cannot deny their evidence. Why then do you indulge in all this vain talk?

At this point in the Book of Job as we have it a third cycle of speeches commences, which has suffered a great deal of dislocation so that editors have had to reassign passages to different speakers. But some points emerge clearly. Eliphaz now says that he is convinced that Job must have committed grave misdeeds and in fact goes on to catalogue them. He *must* have done these evil things—he has oppressed the poor, refused food and drink to the hungry, sent widows and orphans away empty-handed. God has seen all this and has punished him. Then, in what is almost a parody of the great Old Testament prophets' pleas to the people of Israel to repent of their sins and return to the Lord, he goes on to beseech Job to return to the Almighty and put away his unrighteousness. If he does so, all will be well with him. Job's reply again presents his complaint that he is given no opportunity of presenting his case before God. His search for a confrontation with God gets steadily more passionate:

> Oh that I knew where I might find him,
> That I might come even to his seat!

But wherever he may go, he cannot see him. God remains in darkness. On earth the rich oppress the poor and a great cry rises up from the oppressed, but God seems to think nothing wrong. Murderers, thieves, and adulterers flourish. In the end, all die. There follows a fine poetic evocation of God's power as evinced in nature that seems to belong to Bildad although in the text as we have it it is attributed to Job, another account of the doom of the wicked that seems to belong to Zophar, the splendid poem on Wisdom, an independent poem that has got into the Book of Job either by deliberate insertion or in some other way, and a speech of Job full of nostalgia for the days of his prosperity and happiness. Finally, Job delivers his last great speech of self-vindication, consisting of a series of what are known as "oaths of clearance." He swears that he has not committed any of the crimes he lists. This speech has been called Job's "Code of a Man of Honour." He has always dealt generously and properly with women, he has dealt fairly with servants, he has been considerate towards the poor and helped the widow and the orphan, for he has always been aware of the basic equality of all human beings. He has never been proud or complacent with respect to his wealth. He has never acted deceitfully. He has been generous to his enemies and has never turned away a stranger from his door. He concludes:

> Oh that I had one to hear me!
> Behold my signature, let the Almighty answer me,
> And let my adversary write a document.

The last line means "let the prosecutor draw up his indictment." The traditional rendering, "Oh that mine adversary had written a book," obscures the legal implication of the wish. The word rendered "adversary" is אִישׁ רִיבִי—"the man of my dispute," "the man of my law-case," his opponent or prosecutor in a court of law. It is Job's final demand for a confrontation with God.

At this point in the text as we have it there come the speeches of Elihu, a newcomer to the scene. Almost all scholars see this as a later interpolation, and I am sure that it is. It certainly interferes with the tremendous dramatic impact of the theophany, which should surely follow immediately on Job's ending his speeches. "The words of Job are ended," is how he concludes his last speech. Then suddenly (if we omit the Elihu interpolation) Job gets, in a quite unexpected way, the confrontation with God that he has been demanding. It is overwhelming. In an outburst of spectacular cosmic poetry the voice of God hammers home the point that the goings-on in the universe are far beyond the wit of man to comprehend; that nature was not created for man and has its otherness and its mysteries that man can never penetrate; and it is against this background of miracle and mystery which dwarfs man that the problems of human suffering must be set. The Authorized Version communicates the power and the poetry of the divine declaration, although sometimes we may prefer a more pithy statement, such as Pope's "Tell me, if you know so much" for the Authorized Version's "Declare, if thou hast understanding." But here is how it begins:

Then the Lord answered Job out of the whirlwind, and said,

Who is this that darkeneth counsel
By words without knowledge?

Gird up now thy loins like a man;
For I will demand of thee, and answer thou me.

Where was thou when I laid the foundations of the earth?
Declare, if thou hast understanding.

Who hath laid the measures thereof, if thou knowest?
Or who hath stretched the line upon it?

Whereupon are the foundations thereof fastened?
Or who laid the corner-stone thereof?

When the morning stars sang together,
And all the sons of God shouted for joy?

Or who shut up the sea with doors,
When it broke forth, as if it had issued out of the womb?

When I made the cloud the garment thereof,
And thick darkness and swaddling-band for it,

And brake up for it my decreed place,
And set bars and doors,

And said, Hitherto shalt thou come, but no further;
And here shall thy proud waves be stayed?

> Hast thou commanded the morning since thy days,
> And caused the dayspring to know his place;
>
> That it might take hold of the ends of the earth,
> That the wicked might be shaken out of it?

The divine voice goes on and on, insisting again and again on the mysterious dimensions of the universe.

> Hast thou perceived the breadth of the earth?
> Declare, if thou knowest it all.

The nature of light, the coming of rain, desert and blossoming ground— these and other natural mysteries are presented in a series of what almost might be called bullying rhetorical questions:

> Hath the rain a father?
> Or who hath begotten the drops of dew?
>
> Out of whose womb came the ice?
> And the hoar-frost of heaven, who hath gendered it? . . .
>
> Canst thou bind the chains of the Pleiades,
> Or loose the bands of Orion?
>
> Canst thou bring forth Mazzaroth in his season?
> Or canst thou guide Arcturus with his sons?
>
> Knowst thou the ordinances of heaven?
> Canst thou set the dominion thereof in the earth?

The voice goes on to ask whether Job understands how lions hunt, how lion cubs get their food, how the raven is provided for, at what time wild goats bear their young. The natural world is full of wonders which have nothing to do with man. It is in this context that we get the famous description of the war-horse:

> Hast thou given the horse strength?
> Hast thou clothed his neck with thunder? . . .
>
> He paweth in the valley, and rejoiceth in his strength:
> He goeth on to meet the armed men.
>
> He mocketh at fear, and is not affrighted;
> Neither turneth he back from the sword . . .
>
> He swalloweth the ground with fierceness and rage:

Neither believeth he that it is the sound of the trumpet.

He saith among the trumpets, Ha, ha;
And he smelleth the battle afar off,
The thunder of the captains, and the shouting.

This is Job's answer from God.

Moreover the Lord answered Job, and said,

Shall he that contendeth with the Almighty instruct him?
He that reproveth God, let him answer it.

Job is hammered into submission. He replies (and I am modifying the Authorized Version here):

Behold, I am of small account; how can I answer thee?
I lay my hand upon my mouth.

Once have I spoken, but I will not answer again;
Yea, twice, but I will proceed no further.

God, however, brushes aside Job's submissive reply and goes on to bombard him further with rhetorical questions illustrating God's power and the unfathomable mysteries of the universe he created. But also for the first time there is something that sounds very like an implicit admission that evil exists in the world and God has not been able to conquer it fully. After throwing at Job the questions

Wilt thou also make void my judgement?
Wilt thou condemn me, that thou mayst be justified?

Hast thou an arm like God?
Or canst thou thunder with a voice like him?

God goes on to ask Job if he, Job, can cope with the problem of putting the wicked in his place. If Job can do that

Then will I also confess unto thee
That thine own right hand can save thee.

It is almost as though God is saying that He, God, finds the problem of evil intractable, and that if Job can solve it, he can take over. But the thought is not lingered over, for the voice goes on immediately to one of the most powerful and memorable of all the descriptions in these divine speeches, the account of Behemoth (which some commentators take to be the hippopotamus and others to be a purely mythical monster) and Leviathan (sometimes held to denote the crocodile but more likely also a mythical monster). The pictures given here of wondrous beasts leading their own strange lives with their enormous size and total imperviousness to any human attempt to control them once more stress that the universe was not created for man, that there are elements in it far from his concerns, his power, and his comprehension. The poetic imagery in these passages is positively startling, and the range of vocabulary remarkable.

Job's questions concern the relation between power and justice. They are not directly answered by the divine voice. Ethical questions are answered by—almost, one might say, are subsumed in—natural description. What emerges is that the only real answer to Job's question is that there is no answer. The universe is more complicated than man can ever hope to understand, so he had better refrain from discussing the principles on which it is run. The position taken up here is totally opposed to the Wordsworthian view of Nature, that has had so much influence on the British imagination. The mind of man and principles of Nature are not intimately fitted to each other, as Wordsworth believed. There are no moral principles to be deduced from Nature, and no comfort to be derived from it, apart from the dubious comfort of realizing its mysterious otherness. This sense of the otherness of the natural world appears intermittently in later European literature; it is given splendid expression on Hugh MacDiarmid's *On a Raised Beach;* but it can hardly be said to play a central part in the European literary imagination.

At the end of God's second speech Job submits. He has had his confrontation and there is no more to say. But then comes the surprise. The divine voice turns to Eliphaz. "My wrath is kindled against thee and against thy two friends: for ye have not spoken of me the thing that is right, as my servant Job hath." The repetition of pious platitudes about the wicked being punished and the righteous rewarded, and the inference that prosperity indicates virtue and suffering indicates sin are offensive to God. Job may have been rash and arrogant to challenge God to an explanation, but at least in doing so he showed his awareness of the mysteries and paradoxes of God's creation. God's reply emphasizes the mystery and the paradox. Man must recognize them, but he must accept that he cannot fathom them. The solution to Job's problem, in fact, is subsumed in *wonder.*

There are some apparent contradictions in all this. God simultaneously reproves Job for speaking in ignorance and says that he is right in what he says about God. The Hebrew word here rendered as "right" is *nechonah*, correct. Is the implication that it is correct to challenge neat traditional views about God's ways even though the challenger is bound to be ignorant of what really lies behind those ways? Perhaps so. But it is interesting that this coda, which follows God's speeches and Job's submission, is in prose, not poetry, and precedes the prose folktale conclusion in which Job is restored to more than his former good fortune.

The real theodicy is in the words of the divine voice. But is it really a justification of the ways of God to men? Nothing is said about God's justice. The problem remains insoluble. Certainly Milton, who knew and admired the Book of Job and regarded it as a "brief epic," cannot have regarded it as a satisfactory justification of the ways of God to men.

Truth and Poetry in the Book of Job

Robert Alter

The power of Job's unflinching argument, in the biblical book that bears his name, has rarely failed to move readers, but the structure of the book has been a perennial puzzle. It begins, as we all recall, with a seemingly naive tale: Job is an impeccably God-fearing man, happy in his children and in his abundant possessions. Unbeknownst to him, in the celestial assembly the Adversary—despite the translations, not yet a mythological Satan—challenges God to test the disinterestedness of Job's piety by afflicting him. When Job, in rapid succession, has been bereft of all his various flocks and servants and then of all his children, and is stricken from head to foot with itching sores, he refuses his wife's urging that he curse God and die but instead sits down in the dust in mournful resignation.

At this point, the prose of the frame-story switches into altogether remarkable poetry. The poetic Job begins by wishing he had never been born. Then, in three long rounds of debate, he confronts the three friends who have come with all the assurance of conventional wisdom to inform him that his suffering is certain evidence of his having done evil. Job consistently refuses to compromise the honesty of his own life, and in refuting the friends' charges he repeatedly inveighs against God's crushing unfairness. Eventually, the Lord answers Job out of a whirlwind, mainly to show how presumptuous this human critic of divine justice has been. Job concedes; the prose frame-

From *The Art of Biblical Poetry.* © 1985 by Robert Alter. Basic Books, 1985.

story then clicks shut by restoring to Job health, wealth, and prestige, at the same time symmetrically providing him with another set of children.

This ending has troubled many readers over the centuries. Even if we put aside the closing of the folktale frame, so alien to later sensibilities in its schematic doubling of lost property and its simple replacement of lost lives, the Voice from the Whirlwind (or more properly, Storm) has seemed to some a rather exasperating answer to Job's anguished questions. The common objection to what is clearly intended as a grand climax of the poetic argument runs along the following lines: The Voice's answer is no answer at all but an attempt to overwhelm poor Job by an act of cosmic bullying. Job, in his sense of outrage over undeserved suffering, has been pleading for simple justice. God ignores the issue of justice, not deigning to explain why innocent children should perish, decent men and woman writhe in affliction, and instead sarcastically asks Job how good *he* is at hurling lightning bolts, making the sun rise and set, causing rain to fall, fixing limits to the breakers of the sea. The clear implication is that if you can't begin to play in My league, you should not have the nerve to ask questions about the rules of the game.

Some modern commentators have tried to get around such objections by arguing that the very inadequacy of the solution to the problem of theodicy at the end of Job is a testimony to the integrity of the book and to the profundity with which the questions have been raised. There is, in other words, no neat way to reconcile ethical monotheism with the fundamental fact that countless innocents suffer terrible fates through human cruelty, blind circumstance, natural disaster, disease, and genetic mishap. Rather than attempt a pat answer, then, the Job poet was wise enough to imply that there could be no real answer and that the sufferer would have to be content with God's sheer willingness to express His concern for His creatures. This reading of the Voice from the Whirlwind is up to a point plausible, but it may glide too easily over the fact that God's speeches at the end have, after all, a specific content, which is articulated with great care and to the details of which we are presumably meant to attend carefully.

It has also been suggested that the "solution" to Job's dilemma is in the essential act of revelation itself, whatever we think about what is said. That does seem a very biblical idea. Job never doubts God's existence, but, precisely because he assumes in biblical fashion that God must be responsible for everything that happens in the world, he repeatedly wants to know why God now remains hidden, why He does not come out and confront the person on whom He has inflicted such acute suffering. The moment the Voice begins to address Job out of the storm, Job already has his answer: that, despite appearances to the contrary, God cares enough about man to reveal Himself to humankind, to give man some intimation of the order and direction of His creation.

This proposal about the importance of revelation at the end brings us a little closer, I think, to the actual intent of the two climactic divine discourses. What needs to be emphasized, however, considerably more than has been done, is the essential role poetry plays in the imaginative realization of revelation. If the poetry of Job—at least when its often problematic text is fully intelligible—looms above all other biblical poetry in virtuosity and sheer expressive power, the culminating poem that God speaks out of the storm soars beyond everything that has preceded it in the book, the poet having wrought a poetic idiom even richer and more awesome than the one he gave Job. Through this pushing of poetic expression toward its own upper limits, the concluding speech helps us see the panorama of creation, as perhaps we could do only through poetry, with the eyes of God.

I realize that this last assertion may sound either hazily mystical or effusively hyperbolic, but what I am referring to is an aspect of the book that seems to have been knowingly designed by the poet and that to a large extent can be grasped, as I shall try to show, through close analytic attention to formal features of the poem. The entire speech from the storm not only is an effectively structured poem in itself but is finely calculated as a climactic development of images, ideas, and themes that appear in different and sometimes antithetical contexts earlier in the poetic argument. In saying this, I do not by any means intend to dismiss the scholarly consensus that there are composite elements in the Book of Job, that it is not all the work of one hand. The most visible "seams" in the book are between the frame-story and the poetic argument, but this evident disjuncture is not really relevant to our concern with the Voice from the Whirlwind, and it makes little difference whether one regards the frame-story as an old folktale incorporated by the poet or (my own preference) as an old tradition artfully reworked by the poet in a consciously archaizing style. Within the poetic argument itself, there is fairly general agreement among scholars that the Hymn to Wisdom, which is chapter 28, and the Elihu speeches, chapters 32–37, are interpolations for which the original Job poet was not responsible. I am not inclined to debate either of these judgments, but I should like to observe that the later poet and, in the case of chapter 28, the editor who chose the poem from the literature of Wisdom psalms available to him were so alive to the culminating function of the Voice from the Whirlwind that they justified the inclusion of the additional material at least in part as anticipations of the concluding poem. In fact, the claim made by some scholars that chapters 38–41 are themselves an addition to the original text seems to me quite inadmissible precisely because the poetry of this final speech is so intricately and so powerfully a fulfillment of key elements in the body of the poetic argument.

There are, to begin with, occasional and significant adumbrations of the cosmic perspective of God at the end in the speeches of both Job and the friends. Sometimes, in the case of the friends, this is simply a matter of getting divine knowledge backward. Thus Eliphaz, in a speech asserting complacent confidence that God invariably destroys the evil man, draws an analogy from the animal kingdom: "Roar of the lion, voice of the cub, / but the king-of-beasts' teeth are broken. // The lion perishes lacking prey, / and its whelps are scattered" (4:10–11). The point, presumably, is that in God's just world even the fiercest of ravening beasts can be disabled, as seemingly powerful evil-doers in the human sphere will get their comeuppance. But this is to draw a general moral rule from a rare zoological case, and when God Himself evokes the lion (38:39) along with other beasts of prey, He recognizes unflinchingly that the real principle of the animal kingdom is that the strong devour the weak to sustain their own lives and those of their young. It is that harsher, more unassimilable truth that He chooses to make an integral part of His revelation to Job concerning the providential governance of the world.

More frequently, the friends, as self-appointed defenders of God's position, touch on certain notions that are actually in consonance with the divine speech at the end, but both the terms in which such notions are cast and the contexts in which they are set turn them into some-thing jejune and superficial. In this regard, the Voice from the Whirl-wind is a revelation of the contrast between the jaded half-truths of cliché and the startling, difficult truths exposed when the stylistic and conceptual shell of cliché is broken open. Thus Eliphaz, in one of the friends' frequent appeals to the antiquity of received wisdom, upbraids Job: "Are you the first man to be born, / were you spawned before the hills? // Have you attended to the council of God, / and taken to yourself all wisdom?" (15:7–8). Eliphaz's heightening of a sarcastic hyperbole from verset to verset (first born man—created before the world itself—a uniquely privileged member of God's cosmogonic council) leads us to a point in some ways similar to God's overwhelming challenge to Job at the beginning of His great speech. But Eliphaz invokes creation in the smoothly formulaic language of poetic tradition, which is quite different from the vertiginous vision of the vastness of creation that God's bolder language will offer. And Eliphaz speaks smugly without suspecting that there might be a chasm between divine knowledge and the conventional knowledge of accepted wisdom. This immediately becomes clear as he goes on to reduce his cosmogonic hyperbole to a mere competition of longevity with Job: "What do you know that we don't know, / or understand that we do not? // There are grayheads and old men among us, / older by far than your father" (15:9–10).

A little earlier, there is a speech of Zophar's that sounds even more like an anticipation of the Voice from the Whirlwind, but again the stylistic and attitudinal differences between human and divine discourse are crucially instructive.

> Can you find out the limit of God,   the last reaches of the Almighty
>   can you find?
> With the heights of the heavens   what's deeper than Sheol, how can
>   what can you do,   you know?
> Longer than earth is its measure,   and broader than the sea.
>
>   (11:7–9)

In the biblical way of thinking, all this is unexceptionable, and it would seem to accord perfectly with God's own words in chapter 38 about the unbridgeable gap between powerful Creator and limited creature. But the very smoothness of the stereotyped language Zophar uses (heights of heaven, depths of Sheol, longer than earth, broader than the sea) is a clue that this is a truth he has come by all too easily. This suspicion is confirmed when he immediately proceeds to move from an affirmation of God's power to the usual pat assertion that the all-knowing Creator detects all evil—by implication, to chastise the evildoers: "If He goes by and confines, or calls together, who can turn Him back? // For He knows the deceitful, / when He sees iniquity, does He not discern it?" (11:10–11). The actual prospect of God as sole master of the heights of heaven and the depths of hell is a staggering one, as the Voice from the Whirlwind will make awesomely clear. But in Zophar's speech there is too facile a transition from the invocation of that prospect to the timeworn notion that God will never allow crime to pay.

In Job's complaint there are two extended anticipations of the Voice from the Whirlwind, 9:5–10 and 12:7–25. For the sake of economy, I shall cite only the first, and shorter, of these two passages, with brief reference to the second. Job, in the midst of objecting that God is an impossible legal adversary because He is so overpowering, shifts his imagery upward from the arena of law to the cosmos:

Who tears up mountains that know not,	Who overturns them in His wrath,
Who shakes earth from its place,	so that its pillars quake,
Who orders the sun not to rise,	Who seals up the stars,
Who stretched out the heavens alone,	and trod on the back of the sea,
Who made the Bear and Orion,	Pleiades and the chambers of the south wind,
Who does great things without limit,	wonders without number.

Job's cosmic poetry, unlike that of the friends, has a certain energy of vision, as though it proceeded from some immediate perception of the great things it reports. Most of the images he uses will reappear, more grandly, in God's first discourse in chapter 38. There, too, God is the sole sovereign of the sun and the stars, the master of the very constellations and of the chambers of the wind mentioned here. There is, nevertheless, a decisive difference in emphasis between the two chapters, which leads me to infer that this and other passages in the poetic argument are in one respect patiently teaching us how to read God's speech when it finally comes. The Creator in chapter 38 is distinguished by His ability to impose order. The Creator in Job's poem is singled out first of all for His terrific, and perhaps arbitrary, power— tearing up mountains in His wrath, eclipsing the sun, and blotting out the stars. (The speaker, we should remember, is the same Job who had prayed for every glimmer of light to be swallowed by darkness.) If both the present text and chapter 38 allude indirectly to the Canaanite creation myth, in which the land god conquers the primordial sea beast Yam, what is stressed in chapter 38 is God's setting limits to the breakers of the sea, His bolting doors against the chaotic rush of the flood, while Job here gives us instead God the mighty combatant, treading on the back of the conquered sea. To be sure, there is also an element of celebration of the Creator in Job's words, at least in the last two lines of the passage quoted, but his general perception of the master of the universe is from the viewpoint of someone who has been devastated by His mastery. This sense is made perfectly clear in the lines that introduce our passage (9:2–3), and the point is even more emphatic in the lines that follow it: "Why, He snatches—who can turn Him back? / Who can tell Him, 'What are You doing?' // God will not turn back His wrath, / beneath Him sink the Sea Beast's allies" (9:12–13).

The analogous passage in chapter 12 stresses still more boldly the arbitrary way in which God exercises His power. Here, too, God, as in the revelation from the storm at the end, is imagined as the supreme master of nature—a truth that, according to Job, we can learn from the very birds of the heavens and the beasts of the field (*behemot,* a term that in a different acceptation will designate one of the featured attractions of the grand zoological show in the speech from the storm). And like the Lord Who will reveal Himself in the end to Job, God here is imagined above all as the absolute sovereign of light and darkness: "Who lays bare deep things from darkness, / and brings out to light the gloom" (12:22). But this divine monarch as Job conceives Him shows a singular inclination to capricious behavior, befuddling counselors and judges, unmanning kings, humiliating nobles, using His prerogative over light and darkness to draw the leaders of nations into trackless wastes: "They grope in darkness without light, / He makes them stray as though drunk" (12:25). Job's vision of God's power over the world has an authority lacking in the parallel speeches of the friends, but he sees it as power willfully misused, and that perception will require an answer by the Voice from the Whirlwind.

Somewhat surprisingly, the two extended anticipations of the concluding poem that show the greatest degree of consonance with it occur in the presumably interpolated passages, the Elihu speech and the Hymn to Wisdom. This may seem less puzzling if we remember that in the ancient Near East a "book" remained for a long time a relatively open structure, so that later writers might seek to amplify or highlight the meaning of the original text by introducing materials that reinforced or extended certain of the original emphases. In the case of Elihu, the immediate proximity to God's speech is the most likely explanation of the high degree of consonance with it. That is, Elihu is an irascible, presumptuous blowhard (images of inflation and evacuation cluster at the beginning of his discourse), and as such he is hardly someone to be in any way identified as God's "spokesman." But as he approaches the end of his long harangue—as the poem draws close, in other words, to the eruption of the Voice from the Whirlwind—he begins to weave into his abuse of Job images of God as the mighty sovereign of a vast creation beyond the ken of man. First he conjures up a vision of God Whose years are without number mustering the clouds and causing the rains to fall (37:26–33). Then, at the very end of his speech, in a clear structural bridge to the divine discourse that directly follows, Elihu asks Job whether he can really grasp God's wondrous management of the natural world, invoking it as evidence of the moral perfection of the Divinity that man cannot fathom:

Give ear to this, Job,	stop and consider the wonders of God.
Do you know what God sets on them,	when He makes His thunderheads glow?
Do you know in the cloud-expanses	the wonders of the Perfect in Knowledge?
Why your clothes are hot	when earth is becalmed from the south?
Can you beat flat the skies with Him,	firm as a molten mirror?
Let us know what to say to Him,	we can make no case from darkness.
Will it be told Him if I speak,	can man say if he is distraught?
Now, one sees not the light,	though bright in the skies,
till a wind comes and clears them.	
From the north gold comes,	around God awesome the splendor.
The Almighty—we attain Him not—lofty in power,	justice and great right He will not pervert.
So men fear Him,	no wise man can see Him.

(37:14–24)

Elihu's cosmic poetry does not quite soar like that of the Voice from the Whirlwind (and this passage also involves several textual difficulties), but it is considerably more than the rehearsal of formulas we saw in Eliphaz and Zophar. The various items of his panorama of creation—the power over rain and thunder and the dazzling deployment of sunlight—will in a moment recur, more grandly, in God's speech, and, above all, the final emphasis on man's inability to see the solar brilliance of the all-powerful God points toward the extraordinary exercise of divine sight in which we are privileged to share through the poetry of God's concluding speech.

The Hymn to Wisdom, chapter 28, is in certain obvious ways cut from different cloth from the rest of the Book of Job. Lexically and stylistically, it sounds more like Proverbs than Job. Its celebration of divine Wisdom does not at all participate in the vehement argument on theodicy into which it is introduced. Structurally, the hymn is divided into three strophes of approximately equal length with the boundaries between them marked by a refrain; such explicit symmetry of form is not observable elsewhere in the poetry of Job. The imagery of precious stones that dominates the middle strophe has very few parallels elsewhere in the book. But all these disparities may have troubled the ancient audience a good deal less than they trouble us, with our notions of literary unity based on the reading of unitary texts produced by single authors who generally could be fully responsible for them from first draft to corrected page proofs. Whatever editor or ancient literary gremlin decided to insert this poem just after the completion of the rounds of debate with the friends and before Job's final Confession of Innocence (chaps. 29–31) chose the new material with a firm sense of how it could help tune up the proper attentiveness for God's concluding speech. That tuning up is a matter not just of emphasizing the vast scope of God's Wisdom against man's limited understanding but also of poetically defining a *place* where we can begin to imagine the unfathomable workings of the Creator. A whole world of sprawling expanses and inaccessible depths and heights is evoked in the poem—"A path unknown to the hawk, / ungrazed by the falcon's eye" (28:7), unguessed realms of hidden recesses that only God can see or bring to light if He chooses. The thematic stress on sight intimated at the end of the Elihu speeches is prominent here and made powerfully explicit in the concluding strophe. At the same time, specific details of the cosmic imagery that will begin the divine discourse are strategically anticipated (or, to think in the order of the editorial process rather than in the sequential order of the book, are strategically echoed):

And Wisdom, from where does it come,	where is the place of understanding?
It is hidden from the eyes of all living,	from the birds of the heavens concealed.
Perdition and Death say,	"With our ears we but heard its report."
God understands its way,	He knows its place.
For He looks to the ends of the earth,	all beneath heaven He sees,
Fixing a weight to the wind,	setting a measure to water,
When He fixed a limit to the rain,	and a way to the thunderstorm,
Then he saw and gauged it,	set it firm and probed it out.

And said to man,   Look, fear of the Lord is Wisdom,
        and to shun evil is understanding.

(28:20–28)

The aphoristic concluding line is distinctly unlike the Voice from the Whirlwind not merely stylistically but also in the neatness of its sense of resolution. (Its formulaic pairing, however, of "wisdom" and "understanding" is quite like the one God invokes in His initial challenge to Job.) In any case, the discrepancy in tone and attitude of the last line was no doubt far less important to whoever was responsible for the text of Job as we have it than the consonance of the hymn's vision of God with the Voice from the Whirlwind—that is, a vision of God as the master of sight, searching out the unknowable ends of the earth.

How are the resources of poetry marshaled in the divine speech to give us an intimation of that omniscient perspective? Some preliminary remarks on the progression of the concluding poem may help indicate where it means to take us. The structure of the poem is expansive and associative (quite unlike the tight organization of chapter 28), but it also reflects the sequential and focusing strategies of development that are generally characteristic of biblical poetry. After the two brief opening lines in which the Lord challenges Job (38:2–3), the poem leads us through the following movements: cosmogony (38:4–21), meteorology (38:22–38), zoology (38:39–39:30). This sequence is implicitly narrative: first God creates the world, then He sets in motion upon it an intricate interplay of snow and rain and lightning and winds, and in this setting He looks after the baffling variety of wild creatures that live on the earth. God's first discourse is followed at the beginning of chapter 40 by a brief exchange between a reprimanding Lord and a humbled Job (40:1–5), and then the beginning of the second discourse, which again challenges Job to gird up his loins and see if he can really contend with God (40:6–13). (Scholarship has generally detected a scrambling or duplication of texts in these thirteen verses, but I find that the various conjectural attempts to reassemble the text create more problems than they solve, while the lines as we have them do not substantially affect the larger structure of the poem.) In the second discourse, we continue with the zoological interests that take up the last half of the first discourse. In accordance, however, with the impulse of heightening and focusing that informs so much of biblical poetry, the second discourse is not a rapid poetic catalogue of animals, like the last half of the first discourse, but instead an elaborate depiction of just two exotic

beasts, the hippopotamus and the crocodile, who are rendered, moreover, in the heightened and hyperbolic terms of mythology as Behemoth and Leviathan.

These are the broad structural lines of the concluding poem, but in
order to understand how it works so remarkably as a "revelation," in
both the ordinary and the theological sense of the term, it is important
to see in detail how its language and imagery flow directly out of the
poetic argument that has preceded. I shall quote in full the first two
movements of cosmogony and meteorology, then refer without full
citation to the naturalistic zoology before attending to the mythopoeic
zoology at the end. Since the verse divisions here correspond precisely
to the line division, I shall use the conventional verse numbers, starting
with verse 2 of chapter 38, where the poem proper begins.

2 Who is this darkening counsel   in words without knowledge?
3 Gird up your loins like a man,   I'll ask you, and you may inform
                                    Me.
4 Where were you when I   Tell, if you know understanding.
   founded earth?
5 Who set its measures, do you   Or who stretched the line upon it?
   know?
6 In what were its bases sunk,   or who laid its cornerstone,
7 When the morning stars sang   all the sons of God shouted for joy?
   together,
8 Hedged the sea in with doors,   when it gushed forth from the
                                    womb,
9 When I made cloud its clothing,   deep mist its swaddling bands,

10 Placed on it breakers as My   set up bolt and doors.
   limit,
11 I said, "Thus far come, no   here halt the surge of your waves."
   farther,
12 Did you ever muster the   appoint dawn to its place,
   morning,
13 To seize the corners of the   that the wicked be shaken from it?
   earth,
14 It turns like sealing clay   till fixed like [the hues of] a
                                 garment.
15 Their light is withheld from   the upraised arm is broken.
   the wicked,
16 Have you come to the depths   at the ends of the deep walked
   of the sea,   about?
17 Have the gates of death been   the gates of gloom have you seen?
   shown you,

18 Can you take in the breadth of the earth?   Tell, if you know it all.

19 Where is the way light dwells,   and darkness, where is its place,

20 That you may take it to its home,   understand the paths to its house?

21 You know, for you were then born,   the number of your days is great.

22 Have you come into the storehouse of snows,   the storehouse of hail have you seen,

23 Which I set aside for time of strife,   the day of war and battle?

24 By what way is the west wind spread,   the east wind whipped across earth?

25 Who cut the torrent a channel,   a way for the thunderstorm?

26 To rain upon land without man,   wilderness without human soul,

27 To sate the wild wasteland,   and make the grass sprout there?

28 Does the rain have a father,   or who sired the drops of dew?

29 From whose belly did the ice come forth,   to the frost of heaven who gave birth?

30 Like stone water congeals,   the face of the deep locks hard.

31 Can you tie bands to the Pleiades,   or loose Orion's reins?

32 Can you bring out Mazarot in season,   conduct the Bear with its cubs?

33 Do you know the laws of the heavens,   can you fix their rule on earth?

34 Can you lift your voice to the cloud,   and the water-spate covers you?

35 Can you order the lightning to go,   make it say, "Here I am"?

36 Who put wisdom in the hidden parts,   who gave the mind understanding?

37 Who told the heavens in wisdom,   the bottles of the heavens who tipped down?

38 When dust melts to a mass,   and clods clump together.

At the very beginning of the poetic argument, we entered the world of Job's inner torment through the great death-wish poem that takes up all of chapter 3. These first thirty-seven lines of God's response to Job constitute a brilliantly pointed reversal, in structure, image, and theme, of that initial poem of Job's. Perhaps the best way to sense the special weight of the disputation over theodicy is to observe that it is cast in the form of a clash between two modes of poetry, one kind spoken by man and, however memorable, appropriate to the limitations of his creaturely condition, the other the kind of verse a poet of genius could persuasively imagine God speaking. The poem of chapter 3, as we had occasion to see in detail, advanced through a process of focusing in and in—or, to shift metaphors, a relentless drilling inward toward the unbearable core of Job's suffering, which he imagined could be blotted out by extinction alone. The external world—dawn and sunlight and starry night—exists in these lines only to be canceled. Job's first poem is a powerful, evocative, authentic expression of man's essential, virtually ineluctable egotism: the anguished speaker has seen, so he feels, all too much, and he wants now to see nothing at all, to be enveloped in the blackness of the womb/tomb, enclosed by dark doors that will remain shut forever. In direct contrast to all this withdrawal inward and turning out of lights, God's poem is a demonstration of the energizing power of panoramic vision. Instead of the death wish, it affirms from line to line the splendor and vastness of life, beginning with a cluster of arresting images of the world's creation and going on to God's sustaining of the world in the forces of nature and in the variety of the animal kingdom. Instead of a constant focusing inward toward darkness, this poem progresses through a grand sweeping movement that carries us over the length and breadth of the created world, from sea to sky to the unimaginable recesses where snow and winds are stored, to the lonely wastes and craggy heights where only the grass or the wildest of animals lives. In Job's initial poem, various elements of the larger world were introduced only as reflectors or rhetorical tokens of his suffering. When the world is seen here through God's eyes, each item is evoked for its own sake, each existing thing having its own intrinsic and often strange beauty. In chapter 3, Job wanted to reduce time to nothing and contract space to the small, dark compass of the locked womb. God's poem by contrast moves through aeons from creation to the inanimate forces of nature to the teeming life on earth and, spatially, in a series of metonymic links, from the uninhabited wasteland (26) to the mountain habitat of the lion and the gazelle (the end of chapter 38 and the beginning of chapter 39) and the steppes where the wild ass roams.

This general turning of Job's first affirmation of death into an affirmation of life is minutely worked out in the language and imagery of the poem that God speaks. Job's initial poem, we recall, began by setting out the binary opposition between day and night, light and darkness, and then proceeded through an intensifying series of wishes that the light be swallowed up by darkness. The opening verset of God's speech summons Job as someone "*darkening* counsel," and the emphatic and repeated play with images of light and darkness in the subsequent lines makes it clear that this initial characterization of Job is a direct critique of his first speech and all that follows from it. (The allusion here to the poem in chapter 3 is reinforced by the term God uses at the beginning of the second line in addressing Job, *géver,* "man," which also occurs at the beginning of Job's first poem—"the night that said, 'A man has been conceived.'" It is as though God were implying: you called yourself man, *géver,* now gird up your loins like a man and see if you can face the truth.) Job, the Voice from the Whirlwind suggests, has gotten things entirely skewed in regard to the basic ontological constituents of light and darkness. The two in fact exist in a delicate and powerful dialectic beyond the ken of man, and the balance between them is part of the unfathomable beauty of creation. This point is intimated in many of the first thirty-seven lines of the poem and made explicit in verses 19–20: "Where is the way light dwells, / and darkness, where is its place, // That you may take it to its home, / understand the paths to its house?"

Job in chapter 3 prayed for cloud and darkness to envelop the day he was born. Cloud and deep mist reappear here in a startlingly new context, as the matinal blanket over the primordial seas, as the swaddling bands of creation (v. 9). Job wanted "gloom" (*tzalmávet*) to cover his existence; here that term appears as part of a large cosmic picture not to be perceived with mere human eyes: "Have the gates of death been shown you, / the gates of gloom have you seen?" (v. 17). In the one explicitly moral point of theodicy made by the Voice from the Whirlwind (vv. 12–15), the diurnal rhythm of light succeeding darkness is taken as both emblem and instrument of God's ferreting out of evildoers—an idea not present to the "Ecclesiastean" vision of chapter 3, where evil and oppression are merely part of the anguished and futile cyclical movement of life. It is not surprising that this particular passage should be terse and a little cryptic, for whatever God means to suggest about bringing wrongdoing to light, He is not invoking the simple moral calculus used so unquestioningly by the friends. Job in the ascending spirals of his pain-driven rhetoric sought to summon all forms of darkness to eclipse forever the sun and moon and stars. In response God asks him whether he has any notion of what it means in amplitude and moral power to be able to muster the dawn (v. 12) and set the constellations in their regular motion (vv. 31–33).

Perhaps the finest illustration of this nice match of meaning and imagery between the two poems is the beautiful counterbalance between the most haunting of Job's lines wishing for darkness and the most exquisite of God's lines affirming light. Job, one recalls, tried to conjure up an eternal starless night: "Let its twilight stars stay dark, / let it hope for light and have none, / let it not see the eyelids of the dawn" (3:9). God, near the beginning of His first discourse, evokes the moment when creation was completed in an image that has become justly famous in its own right but that is also, it should be observed, a counterimage to 3:9: "When the morning stars sang together, / all the sons of God shouted for joy" (v. 7). That is, instead of a night with no twilight stars, with no glimmer of dawn, the morning stars of creation exult. The emphasis in this line on song and shouts of joy also takes us back to the poem of chapter 3, which began with a triumphant cry on the night of conception—a cry Job wanted to wish away—and proceeded to a prayer that no joyous exclamation come into that night (3:7). Finally, the vestigially mythological "sons of God"—with the semantic breadth in Hebrew of "son," this implies not biological filiation but something like "celestial company"—takes us back beyond chapter 3 to the frame-story. There, of course, it was the Adversary who was the prominent and sinister member of "the sons of God." The discordant note he represented has been expunged here in this heavenly chorus of creation. What I am pointing to is not one of those contradictions of sources on which biblical scholarship has too often thrived but a culminating moment in which the vision of the poet transcends the limited terms of the folktale he has chosen to use.

There is a second set of key images in the first movement of God's speech that harks back to Job's initial poem, namely, the imagery of physical generation and birth. Since this imagery, unlike light and darkness, which are literal substances of creation, is imposed metaphorically by the poet as a way of shaping the material, it provides even clearer evidence of how the poem in chapter 38 was purposefully articulated as a grand reversal of the poem in chapter 3. Job's first speech begins with birth and conception and circles back on the belly or womb where he would like to be enclosed, where he imagines the fate of the dead fetus as the happiest of human lots. Against those doors of the belly (3:10) that Job wanted shut on him forever, the Voice from the Whirlwind invokes a cosmic womb and cosmic doors to a very different purpose: "[He] hedged in the sea with doors, / when it gushed forth from the womb" (v. 8). This figuration of setting limits to the primal sea as closing doors on a gushing womb produces a high tension of meaning absent from Job's unequivocal death wish. The doors are closed and bolted (v. 10) so that the flood will not engulf the earth, but nevertheless the waves surge, the womb of all things pulsates, something is born—a sense made clear in the incipiently narrative development of the womb image into the next line (v. 9), where in a metaphor unique in biblical poetry the primordial mists over the surface of the deep are called swaddling bands.

One might note that in the anticipations of this passage in Job's speech there are allusions to the Canaanite cosmogonic myth of a triumph by force over an archaic sea monster, while in God's own words that martial story is set aside, or at the very least left in the distant background, so that the cosmogony can be rendered instead in terms of procreation. What we are invited to imagine in this fashion is creation not as the laying low of a foe but as the damming up and channeling of powers nevertheless allowed to remain active. (The only clear allusion in the poem to God's doing battle, verse 23, is projected forward in time to an indefinite, perhaps vaguely apocalyptic future.) The poet uses a rather unexpected verb, "to hedge in," in order to characterize this activity of holding back the womb of the sea, and that is a double allusion, to God's protective "hedging round" of Job mentioned in the frame-story and to Job's bitter complaint toward the end of his first poem of having been "hedged in" by God. The verb, in its various conjugations, is nowhere else in the Bible used for the closing of doors but generally suggests a shading or sheltering act, as with a wing or canopy. One usage that might throw some light on our line from Job is this verse in Psalms (139:13): "For You planted conscience within me, / You sheltered me [or, hedged me around, or, wove me] in my mother's belly." The Creator, that is, at the end of Job, is actively blocking off, bolting in, the surge of the sea, but the word carries after it a long train of associations having to do with protection and nurture, so that the negative sense of the verb in chapter 3 is in a way combined with the positive sense in which the frame-story uses it. What results is a virtual oxymoron, expressing a paradoxical feeling that God's creation involves a necessary holding in check of destructive forces and a sustaining of those same forces because they are also forces of life. One sees in a single compact phrase how the terms of God's poetry—which is to say, ultimately, His imagination of the world—transcend the terms of Job's poetry and that of the friends.

When the poem moves on—as I have suggested, in an implicitly narrative movement—from cosmogony to meteorology, birth imagery is once more introduced. First Job is challenged sarcastically, "You know, for you were then born" (v. 21), which, in addition to the ultimate allusion to the beginning of the poem in chapter 3, sounds quite like Eliphaz's words to Job in chapter 15. The crucial difference is that instead of being a rhetorical ploy in a petty contest of supposed longevity, this address is set against a background of cosmic uterine pulsations and leads into a thick cluster of birth images a few lines down (vv. 28–29), so that we quickly grasp the ontological contrast between Job, a man born of woman in time, and the principle of generation infinitely larger than man that informs nature. The two lines below that articulate this principle richly develop the implications of the birth imagery in a characteristically biblical fashion:

Does the rain have a father,   or who sired the drops of dew?
From whose belly did the ice come   to the frost of heaven who gave
    forth,   birth?

In each of these two lines we are carried forward from agent (father) or agency (belly) to the active process of procreation (sired, gave birth—in the Hebrew, two different conjugations of the same verb). Between the first line and the second, what amounts to a biological focusing of the birth image is carried out as we go from the father, the inseminator who is the proximate cause of birth, to the mother, in whose body the actual birth is enacted. The interlinear parallelism of this couplet also plays brilliantly with the two opposed states of water, first liquid and falling or condensing, then frozen. In the first line, the flaunted inapplicability of the birth imagery is a result of multiplicity: How could one imagine anyone fathering the countless millions of raindrops or dewdrops? In the second line, the incongruity—which is to say, the chasm between man's small world and God's vast world—is a more shocking one (still another intensifying development) as the poet's language forces us to imagine the unimaginable, great hunks of ice coming out of the womb. Figurative language is used here to show the limits of figuration itself, which, in the argumentative thrust of the poem, means the limits of the human imagination. The immediately following line (v. 30) is a focusing development of this ice imagery: "Like stone water congeals, / the face of the deep locks hard." The tension of opposites that is at the heart of God's vision of the world is strongly felt here: fluid and stone-hard solid, white-frozen surface and watery depths. Having reached this point, the poet lays aside birth imagery, and after three lines devoted to the stars concludes the whole meteorological segment with a focusing development of the phenomena of natural precipitation we just observed in verses 28–30, which themselves capped a whole sequence on snow and rain that began with verse 22. There remains, of course, an implicit connection between fructification or birth and rain, as anyone living in the Near Eastern climate and topography would be readily aware, and as verse 27 reminds us quite naturalistically and verse 28 by a sort of riddling paradox (no one is the father of the rain, but the rain is the father of life). In any case, the concluding four lines of our segment—putting aside verse 36, whose meaning is uncertain—offer an image of downpour on parched land that is, at least by implication, a final turn of the screw in the poetic rejoinder to chapter 3. In Job's initial poem the only water anywhere in evidence is the saltwater of tears (3:24), and clouds are mentioned only as a means to cover up the light. It is surely appropriate that God should now challenge Job to make lightning leap from the thickness of the cloud and that in His cosmic realm, as against Job's rhetorical realm, the meaning of clouds is not darkness but a source of water to renew the earth with life.

The rest of God's speech—the second half of the first discourse and virtually all of the second discourse—is then devoted to a poetic panorama of the animal life that covers the earth. The sequence of beasts, like the movement of the poem through space via metonymic links, is loosely associative but also instructive: lion, raven, mountain goat and gazelle, wild ass, wild ox, ostrich, war horse, hawk and eagle. The first two and the last two creatures in the sequence are beasts of prey whose native fierceness in effect frames the wildness of the whole catalogue. The sequence begins, that is, with an image of the lion crouching in ambush for its prey (38:39–40), determined to sate its keen appetite; and the sequence closes with this striking evocation of the eagle seeking food for its brood: "From there [the mountain crag] he spies out food, / from afar his eyes discern. // His fledglings gulp blood; / wherever the slain are, there is he" (39:29–30). This concluding poem in Job is probably one of the most unsentimental poetic treatments of the animal world in the Western literary tradition and, at least at first thought, a little surprising coming from the mouth of the Lord. But the violence and, even more, the peculiar beauty of violence are precisely the point of God's visionary rejoinder to Job. The animal realm is a nonmoral realm, but the sharp paradoxes it embodies make us see the inadequacy of any merely human moral calculus—not only that of the friends, learned by rote, but even Job's, spoken out of the integrity of suffering. In the animal kingdom, the tender care for one's young may well mean their gulping the blood of freshly slain creatures. It is a daily rite of sustaining life that defies all moralizing anthropomorphic interpretation. And yet, the series of rhetorical questions to Job suggests, God's providence looks after each of these strange, fierce, inaccessible creatures. There is an underlying continuity between this representation of the animal world and the picture of inanimate nature in 38:2–38, with its sense of terrific power abiding in the natural world, fructification and destruction as alternative aspects of the same, imponderable forces.

That continuity is reinforced by the carryover of images of procreation from the cosmogonic and meteorological sections of the poem to the zoological section. In the two former instances, as we just saw, the language of parturition and progeny was first metaphoric and then both metaphoric and heavily ironic; among the animals, it becomes quite literal. The raven at the beginning of this section (38:41) and the eagle at the end are seen striving to fulfill the needs of their young. Immediately after the raven, the birth process and early growth of the mountain goat and gazelle are given detailed attention:

> Do you know the time when the mountain goat gives birth,
> do you mark the birth pangs of the gazelles?
> Do you number the months till they come to term,
> do you know the time when they give birth?
> They crouch, they push out their young,
> in the throes of labor.
> Their offspring batten, grow large in the wild,
> go off and do not return.
>
> (39:1–4)

The emphasis on time here in conjunction with the evocation of birth brings us back in still another strong antithesis to Job's wish in chapter 3 that he could wipe out his birth. There, one recalls, he cursed the night of his conception by saying, "Let it not come into the number of months" (3:6). Here, in God's poem, that same phrase (with the minor morphological shift in the Hebrew of "number" from noun to verb) recurs as an instance of how time becomes a medium of fruition under the watchful gaze of the divine maker of natural order. Reproduction and nurturing are the very essence of a constantly self-renewing creation as the poet imagines it. But even the universal principle of generation is not free from uncanny contradiction, as the strange case of the ostrich (39:13–18) suggests. That peculiar bird, at least according to the ornithological lore on which the poet drew, abandons her eggs in the dirt, unmindful of the danger that they may be trampled underfoot by wild beasts, "For God deprived her of wisdom, / gave her no share of understanding" (39:17). Nature for the Job poet is not a Newtonian clock operating with automatic mechanisms. The impulse to reproduce and nurture life depends upon God's imbuing each of His creatures with the instinct or "wisdom" to carry it out properly. If the universal provider of life chooses in any case to withhold His understanding—as Job himself is said to lack wisdom and understanding—things can go awry.

In both structure and thematic assertion, chapters 38–41 are a great diastolic movement, responding to the systolic movement of chapter 3. The poetics of suffering in chapter 3 seeks to contract the whole world to a point of extinction, and it generates a chain of images of enclosure and restriction. The poetics of providential vision in the speech from the storm conjures up horizon after expanding horizon, each populated with a new form of life. Thus, in the second segment of the zoological panorama (38:5–12, though in fact cued by 38:4), we see a parade of animals moving outward into the wild, far beyond the yokes and reins of man: first the young of the mountain goats and gazelles, heading out into the open, then the onager and the wild ox that will never be led into a furrow. In chapter 3, only in the grave did prisoners "no longer hear the taskmaster's voice" (3:18), and only there was "the slave free of his master" (3:19). But this, God's rejoinder implies, is a civilization-bound, hobbled perception of reality, for nature abounds in images of freedom: "Who set the wild ass free, / who undid the bonds of the onager, // Whose home I made in the steppes, / his dwelling-place the salt land? // He scoffs at the bustle of the city, / the shouts of the taskmaster he does not hear" (39:5–7).

The way in which these various antitheses between chapter 3 and chapters 38–39 are elaborately pointed may suggest why some of the subsequent major movements in Job's poetic argument are not also alluded to here. In part, the reason might have been a problem of technical feasibility: it is manageable enough to reverse the key-terms and images and themes of one rich poem at the beginning in another poem at the end, but it might have become unwieldy to introduce into the conclusion allusions to a whole series of intervening poems. More substantively, however, God chooses for His response to Job the arena of creation, not the court of justice, the latter being the most insistent recurrent metaphor in Job's argument after chapter 3. And it is, moreover, a creation that barely reflects the presence of man, a creation where human concepts of justice have no purchase. We are accustomed to think of the radicalism of the challenge of God in the Book of Job, but it should be recognized that, against the norms of biblical literature, God's response is no less radical than the challenge. Elsewhere in the Bible, man is the crown of creation, little lower than the angels, expressly fashioned to rule over nature. Perhaps that is why there is so little descriptive nature poetry in the Bible: the natural world is of scant interest in itself; it engages a poet's imagination only insofar as it reflects man's place in the scheme of things or serves his purposes. But in the uniquely vivid descriptive poetry of Job 38–41, the natural world is valuable for itself, and man, far from standing at its center, is present only by implication, peripherally and impotently, in this welter of fathomless forces and untamable beasts.

The most elaborately described as well as the most arresting member of the bestiary in the first discourse is the war-horse. Few readers of the poem would want to give up these splendid lines, though some have wondered what this evocation of the snorting stallion has to do with Job's predicament. Indeed, some have suspected that the vignette of the war-horse, like the clearly related portraits of the hippopotamus and the crocodile in the next two chapters, is really a sort of descriptive set piece which the poet brought in because he knew he could do it so well. It seems to me on the contrary that all three beasts are intrinsically connected with the vision of creation that is God's response to Job's questioning. The stallion enters the poem through a verbal clue: if the foolish ostrich only had wisdom, we are told, it would soar into the sky and "scoff at the horse and its rider" (39:18). This moves us directly into a consideration of the horse, which occupies the penultimate position in the first bestiary, before the concluding image of the eagle that will bring us back in an envelope structure to the initial picture of wild creatures caring for their young:

Do you give the horse his might,   do you clothe his neck with a mane?

Do you make him shake like locusts,   his majestic snorting—terror?

He churns up the valley, exults in power,   goes out toward the weapons.

He scoffs at fear, is undismayed,   turns not back from the sword.

Arrows by the quiverful rattle past him,   the flash of spear and lance.

With clamor and clatter he swallows up ground,   swerves not at the trumpet's blast.

As the trumpet sounds, he says,   From afar he sniffs battle,
  "Aha!"
          the roaring of captains, their shouts.

(39:19–25)

The passage is a rich interweave of heightening maneuvers and narrative developments between versets and between lines, as the war-horse itself is the vivid climactic image of the story the poet has to tell about the animal kingdom—before, that is, Behemoth and Leviathan, who, as we shall see, are a climax beyond the climax. In other words, we perceive the stallion narratively, first snorting and pawing the ground, then dashing into the thick of battle; and we see, for example, his whole body aquiver in a first verset, then a startling focus in the second verset on his nostrils snorting terror. The stallion is a concrete embodiment of contradictions held in high tension, in keeping with the whole vision of nature that has preceded. Though fiercer than the onager and the wild ox, he allows his great power to be subjected to the uses of man; yet, as he is described, he gives the virtual impression of joining in battle of his own free will, for his own pleasure. It would be naïve to conclude from these lines that the poet was interested in promoting martial virtues, but the evoked scene of mayhem does convey a sense that a terrible beauty is born and an awesome energy made manifest in the heat of war. These qualities are continuous with the ravening lion who began the bestiary and with the meteorological poetry before it in which lightning leapt from the cloud and the Lord stored up cosmic weapons in the treasure-houses of snow and hail.

To be sure, the whole zoological section of the poem is meant to tell Job that God's tender mercies are over all His creatures, but tonally and imagistically this revelation comes in a great storm rather than in a still, small voice, for the providence portrayed is over a world that defies comfortable moral categorizings. The most crucial respect in which such defiance makes itself felt is in the immense, imponderable play of power that is seen to inform creation. The world is a constant cycle of life renewing and nurturing life, but it is also a constant clash of warring forces. This is neither an easy nor a direct answer to the question of why the good man should suffer, but the imposing vision of a harmonious order to which violence is nevertheless intrinsic and where destruction is part of creation is meant to confront Job with the limits of his moral imagination, a moral imagination far more honest but only somewhat less conventional than that of the friends. The strange and wonderful description of the hippopotamus and the crocodile, which after the introductory verses of challenge (40:7–14) takes up all of the second discourse, then makes those limits even more sharply evident by elaborating these two climactically focused images of the poem's vision of nature.

There has been a certain amount of quite unnecessary confusion among commentators as to whether the subject of the second discourse is in fact zoology or mythology. Many have argued that the two beasts in question are nothing more than the hippopotamus and the crocodile. Others, like Marvin Pope in his philologically scrupulous treatment of Job, have claimed that both are mythological monsters. "Leviathan" in fact appears in chapter 3 as a mythological entity, and the word is clearly cognate with the Ugaritic Lotan, a kind of sea dragon. The argument for mythology is shakier for Behemoth because there is no extrabiblical evidence of the term as a mythological designation, and all the other occurrences within the Bible would seem to be as a generic term for perfectly naturalistic grass-eating beasts of the field, including an earlier use of the term in Job itself (12:7).

The either/or rigidity of the debate over Behemoth and Leviathan quickly dissolves if we note that these two culminating images of the speech from the storm reflect the distinctive poetic logic for the development of meanings that we have been observing on both small scale and large in biblical poetry. The movement from literal to figurative, from verisimilar to hyperbolic, from general assertion to focused concrete image, is precisely the movement that carries us from the catalogue of beasts to Behemoth and Leviathan. The war-horse, who is the most striking item in the general catalogue and the one also given the most attention quantitatively (seven lines), is a way station in the rising line of semantic intensity that terminates in Behemoth and Leviathan. The stallion is a familiar creature but already uncanny in the beauty of power he represents. From this point, the poet moves on to two exotic animals whose habitat is the banks of the Nile—that is, far removed from the actual experience of the Israelite audience and even farther from that of the fictional auditor Job, whose homeland is presumably somewhere to the east of Israel. The listener, that is, may have actually glimpsed a war-horse or a lion or a mountain goat, but the hippopotamus and crocodile are beyond his geographical reach and cultural ken, and he would most likely have heard of them through travelers' yarns and the fabulation of folklore. The hippopotamus is given ten lines of vivid description that place him on the border between the natural and the supernatural. Not a single detail is mythological, but everything is rendered with hyperbolic intensity, concluding in the strong assertion that no hook can hold him (in fact, the Egyptians used hooked poles to hunt the hippopotamus). The evocation of the crocodile is then accorded thirty-three lines, and it involves a marvelous fusion of precise observation, hyperbole, and mythological heightening of the real reptile, and thus becomes a beautifully appropriate climax to the whole poem.

To put this question in historical perspective, the very distinction we as moderns make between mythology and zoology would not have been so clear-cut for the ancient imagination. The Job poet and his audience, after all, lived in an era before zoos, and exotic beasts like the ones described in chapters 40–41 were not part of an easily accessible and observable reality. The borderlines, then, between fabled report, immemorial myth, and natural history would tend to blur, and the poet creatively exploits this blur in his climactic evocation of the two amphibious beasts that are at once part of the natural world and beyond it.

What is stressed in the description of the hippopotamus is the paradoxical union of pacific nature—he is a herbivore, seen peacefully resting in the shade of lotuses on the riverbank—and terrific power, against which no human sword could prevail. (Thus, whether hippopotami could actually be captured is not important, for the poet needs to drive home the point that this awesome beast is both literally and figuratively beyond man's grasp.) And with strategic effectiveness, the notion of muscular power—bones like bronze, limbs like iron rods—is combined with a striking emphasis on sexual potency, thus extending the images of generation and birth of the first discourse:

> Look, his power is in his loins, his potency in the muscles of his belly.
> He makes his member stand like a cedar, the sinews of his testicles knit together.
>
> (40:16–17)

Biblical poetry in general, certainly when measured by the standard of Greek epic verse, is not very visual, or rather is visual only in momentary flashes and sudden climactic developments. But the description of the crocodile is exceptionally striking in its sustained visual force, in keeping with its role as the culmination of this long, impressive demonstration of God's searching vision contrasted to man's purblind view. I shall translate the last twenty-two lines of the poem, which follow the initial assertion that Leviathan, like Behemoth, is impervious to every hook and snare and every scheme of being subjected to domestication. The line numbers reflect verse numbers in the Hebrew text of chapter 41, beginning with verse 5:

5	Who can uncover his outer garb,	come into his double mail?
6	Who can pry open the doors of his face,	all around his teeth is terror.
7	His back is rows of shields,	closed in a tight seal,
8	One touching the next,	no breath could come between them,
9	Each cleaves to the next,	locked together, they will not part.
10	His sneezes flash light,	his eyes are like the eyelids of the dawn.
11	Firebrands leap from his mouth,	fiery sparks fly off.
12	From his nostrils smoke comes forth,	like a boiling pot on brushwood.
13	His breath kindles coals,	flame comes out of his mouth.
14	Strength dwells in his neck,	before him violence dances.
15	The folds of his flesh cling together,	hard-cast, he will not totter.
16	His heart is cast hard as stone,	cast hard as the nether millstone.
17	When he rears, the gods quail,	when he crashes down, they cringe.
18	No sword that reached him could stand,	neither spear, no dart, nor lance.
19	Iron he deems as straw,	and bronze as rotten wood.
20	No arrow can make him flee,	against him, slingstones turn straw.
21	Missiles are deemed mere straw,	he mocks the javelin's clatter.
22	His underside jagged shards,	he spreads a harrow over mud.
23	He makes the deep seethe like a caldron,	he turns sea to an ointment pan.
24	Behind him glistens a wake,	he makes the depths seem hoary.
25	He has no match on earth,	made as he is without fear.
26	All that is lofty he sees,	he is king over all proud beasts.

The power of the crocodile is suggested both through a heightening of the descriptive terms and through a certain narrative movement. First we get the real beast's awesome teeth and impenetrable armor of scales, then a mythologizing depiction of him breathing smoke and fire and sneezing sparks of light. This representation, moreover, of the fire-breathing beast is strangely reminiscent of the description of the God of battles in 2 Samuel 22 and elsewhere in biblical poetry. At the same time, the series of challenging interrogatives that has controlled the rhetoric of the divine discourse from the beginning of chapter 38 glides into declaratives, starting in verse 7, as the poem moves toward closure.

As elsewhere, the poet works with an exquisite sense of the descriptive needs at hand and of the structural continuities of the poem and the book. The peculiar emphasis on fire and light in the representation of the crocodile takes us back to the cosmic imagery of light in God's first discourse, to the lightning leaping from the cloud, and beyond that to Job's initial poem. In fact, the remarkable and celebrated phrase "eyelids of the dawn," which Job in chapter 3 wanted never to be seen again, recurs here to characterize the light flashing from the crocodile's eyes. This makes us draw a pointed connection and at the same time shows how the poet's figurative language dares to situate rare beauty in the midst of power and terror and strangeness. The implicit narrative development of the description takes us from a vision of the head, armor plate, and body of the beast (vv. 13–24), to a picture of him rearing up and crashing down, brushing off all assailants, and then churning out of our field of vision, leaving behind a foaming wake that, like his mouth and eyes, shines (vv. 25–32). If the language of sea (*yam*) and deep (*tehom, metzulah*) rather than of river water predominates in this final segment, that is in part because of the associations of the mythic Lotan with those terms and that habitat, but also because this vocabulary carries us back to the cosmogonic beginning of God's speech (see in particular 38:16). Job's merely human vision could not penetrate the secrets of the deep, and now at the end we have before our mind's eye the magnificent, ungraspable beast who lives in the deep, who is master of all creatures of land and sea, who from his own, quite unimaginable perspective "sees" all that is lofty. Leviathan is nature mythologized, for that is the poet's way of conveying the truly uncanny, the truly inscrutable, in nature; but he remains part of nature, for if he did not it would make little sense for the poem to conclude, "he is king over all proud beasts."

By now, I would hope it has become clear what on earth descriptions of a hippopotamus and a crocodile are doing at the end of the Book of Job. Obviously, there can be no direct answer to Job's question as to why, having been a decent and God-fearing man, he should have lost all his sons and daughters, his wealth, and his health. Job's poetry was an instrument for probing, against the stream of the friends' platitudes, the depths of his own understandable sense of outrage over what befell him. God's poetry enables Job to glimpse beyond his human plight an immense world of power and beauty and awesome warring forces. This world is permeated with God's ordering concern, but as the vividness of the verse makes clear, it presents to the human eye a welter of contradictions, dizzying variety, energies and entities that man cannot take in. Job surely does not have the sort of answer he expected, but he has a strong answer of another kind. Now at the end he will no longer presume to want to judge the Creator, having been brought through God's tremendous poetry to realize that creation can perhaps be sensed but not encompassed by the mind—like that final image of the crocodile already whipping away from our field of vision, leaving behind only a shining wake for us to see. If Job in his first response to the Lord (40:2, 4–5) merely confessed that he could not hope to contend with God and would henceforth hold his peace, in his second response (42:2–6), after the conclusion of the second divine speech, he humbly admits that he has been presumptuous, has in fact "obscured counsel" about things he did not understand. Referring more specifically to the impact of God's visionary poem, he announces that he has been vouchsafed a gift of sight—the glimpse of an ungraspable creation surging with the power of its Creator: "By what the ear hears I had heard You, / but now my eyes have seen You."

Job's Encounters with the Adversary

Ken Frieden

Although Job has been universally admired, his encounters with evil have met with diverse and often contradictory interpretations. In contrast to the tradition that exalts "patient Job," recent scholars have focused attention on the "impatient Job" who questions divine justice. I will suggest that Job is essentially a book about questions and assertions, a book that leads us to consider the significance of theological questioning.

I

Job raises issues of good and evil, undeserved suffering, and God's justice. Phrased as questions: Is there a force of evil that is independent of God? Why do good people suffer? What can we know about divine justice? But these metaphysical doubts are displaced by a more pragmatic question: How must we act or speak in adversity? In more general terms: What is a right language of relationship to God?

The Book of Job also revolves around several key words: the name "Job," the divine names, and "the adversary" (*ha-satan*). These names denote three different beings and characters in the story, yet they also imply a wider range of meanings. Job's name is close to the Arabic word, *awab,* which connotes one who returns, or turns to God. Yet despite his righteousness, Job finds that evil turns toward him. One Rabbinic interpretation, based on the conviction that everything in

From *Response: A Contemporary Jewish Review* 14, no. 3 (Winter 1985). © 1985 by *Response: A Contemporary Jewish Review.*

Scripture is significant, observes a verbal association: if the middle letters of his name are reversed, Job (*eyov*) becomes an enemy (*oyev*). A chiasmus, here a crossing of good and evil, corresponds to a metathesis, a transposition in the letters of Job's name:

(Chiasmus) Good Job the Upright   [*Eyov*]   (Metathesis)
          Evil Job as Enemy   [*Oyev*]

The crossing of good and evil (or health and sickness, wealth and poverty, nearness to and distance from God) parallels a reversal in the letters of Job's name: *aleph-yud-vav-beth,* approximated in English by e-y-o-v, becomes *aleph-vav-yud-beth,* approximated in English by o-y-e-v. This reversal makes Job, who has always turned toward God, appear to be an enemy of God. After he is initially described as "perfect and upright" (*tam v'yashar*), then the narrative centers on what happens when God appears to treat Job as one would an enemy. The transformation, both experiential and verbal, becomes explicit when Job asks God in chapter 13, verse 24: "Why do you hide your face, / And consider me your enemy?" Of course, Job never actually becomes God's enemy, but must feel that he has, for the purposes of the story. Satan, like language, plays tricks on us.

The name of God also undergoes diverse transformation in the Book of Job: the prologue and epilogue employ the Tetragrammaton (YHWH), while Job only once and his companions never refer to God in this way, instead speaking of *El, Eloah, Elohim,* and *Shaddai.* Some scholars conclude that this is the result of composite authorship, but Rabbinic tradition insists that the different divine names have theological significance. Job's false friends are caught up in misguided assertions about God. Job, in contrast, as he strives to address God, passes through several stages on the way to God's transcendence of language. Although the Tetragrammaton has been translated as "the Lord," these four (now unpronounceable) letters name the ineffable God. The language of Hebrew Scripture preserves a place for what is beyond images and words, the locus of divine mystery.

Ha-satan, the source of our modern Satan, derives from the root *sin-tet-nun,* to act as an adversary, and thus may be translated, "the adversary." The most recent translations printed by the Jewish Publication Society rightly avoid rendering *ha-satan* by the proper name, Satan. Without the definite article, *satan* may be simply "an adversary." The italicized *satan* indicates a Hebrew accent, emphasizing that we are dealing with a key word in a foreign system of beliefs. Unlike the modern Satan, this adversary is not represented as an independent evil being, but rather names a variety of opposing forces. We learn this from the earliest occurrences of the word in Numbers 22:22 and 22:32, when God places an angel in the way of Balaam as a *satan* against him. This *satan* is an adversary or a power of opposition sent by God, and is clearly not independent of Him. The evolution of *satan* and *ha-satan* is worth following through Samuel, Chronicles, and Zechariah, but would lead us too far afield.

In addition to these central themes and key words, what are the essential rhetorical figures in the Book of Job? We may speak of chiasmus, the crossing that makes the upright Job appear to be an enemy of God. But we must especially attend to the tension between conflicting rhetorical modes: question and assertion. Job urges us to consider ways in which men approach God, sharply contrasting Job's form of authentic doubt with his friends' dogmatic statements. The technical term for questioning is "erotesis," from the Greek verb meaning "to question or inquire." The trope or rhetorical device of questioning is, as we will see, even attributed to God in the Book of Job. Whereas assertions imply a situation of monologue in which the listener need not respond, certain questions initiate a dialogue. The Book of Job passes through various forms of questioning, and develops toward an I-Thou relation.

Tropes engender tropes, and no figure of speech stands alone. The rhetoric of questioning is often linked to irony, broadly defined as saying one thing and meaning another. In the Book of Job, we also find quotations and misquotations, both from other works of Near Eastern Wisdom literature and within the book. The situation may be outlined as follows. After the righteous Job loses his children, his possessions, and his health, Job's companions respond to him by compounding the errors of dogmatic theology and misinterpretation. Job, on the other hand, is a probing questioner, so powerful in his questioning that he enters into relationship with God. The differences between Job and his false friends are evident in the language of their debate.

II

Now we can better understand Job's encounters with the adversary. We clearly cannot attempt a comprehensive discussion of Job, but only a close reading of a few central passages. The book opens at an indefinite time and place:

> There was a man in the land of Uz, whose name was Job;
> and that man was perfect and upright, fearing God, and
> turned away from evil. Seven sons and three daughters were
> born to him. His possessions were seven thousand sheep,
> three thousand camels, five hundred yoke of oxen, five
> hundred she-asses, and a very great household; so that this
> man was the greatest of all the children of the east.
>
> (1:1–3)

What is the literary genre of this prologue in prose? "There was a man" sounds like the beginning of a folktale or legend. We know neither when Job lived, nor where Uz was located. Further, Job is described with utmost simplicity, as one who is "perfect and upright" and "the greatest of the sons of the east"; in an ethically reassuring correspondence between virtue and reward, Job is blessed by extreme wealth. Thus Rabbinic tradition notes that Job is no historical person, but rather a typical figure. From the start, we are encouraged to read beyond the literal level of the narrative.

A conflict arises when we learn of Job's children only that they hold feasts:

> His sons used to go and hold a feast in the house of each on
> his day, and they would send and call for their three sisters
> to eat and drink with them. When the feast days had run
> their course, Job sent and sanctified them, rose early in the
> morning, and offered burnt offerings according to the num-
> ber of them all, because Job said: It may be that my children
> have sinned and blessed [a euphemism for "cursed"] God in
> their hearts. Thus Job did continually.
>
> (1:4–5)

The feasts are an incongruous detail for those related to the pious Job. How does he react to their threat to piety? Job keeps his distance from their parties and does not question what they do. Rather than confront them, he seems to turn his back on evil and privately express suspicions. This development gives a new sense to the phrase which describes Job as one who "turned away from evil." We need not say that Job's actions are blameworthy, but that he almost too readily resorts to a ritual act of purification, without entering into a dialogue with his children. The turn away from evil conceals problems that were not immediately apparent.

A parallel scene in heaven immediately follows:

> Now there was a day when the sons of God came to present themselves before God (*YHWH*), and the adversary (*ha-satan*) also came among them.
>
> And God said to the adversary, Whence do you come?
>
> The adversary answered God and said, From deviating (*m'shut*) on the earth and from walking up and down on it.
>
> And God said to the adversary, Have you considered my servant Job, that there is none like him on the earth, a perfect and upright man, fearing God, and turned away from evil?
>
> Then the adversary answered God and said, Does Job fear God for nothing? Have you not made a hedge about him, about his house, and about all that he has, on every side? You have blessed the work of his hands, and his possessions have increased in the land. But now put forth Your hand and touch all that he has, surely he will bless [curse] You to Your face.
>
> And God said to the adversary, Behold, all that he has is in your hands, only against him do not put forth your hand.
>
> And the adversary went out from the presence of God.
>
> (1:6–12)

Whereas Job blesses his children and offers ritual sacrifices, God confronts the adversary. He immediately raises a question that begins a discussion. In response, the adversary also raises questions. But *ha-satan* uses what we loosely call "rhetorical" questions, to which he himself gives answers. Speaking as a prosecuting attorney, the adversary attempts to influence God's judgment of Job. Only God is absolutely justified in employing a mode of assertion, however, as when He describes Job as "fearing God, and turned away from evil." But these words repeat the opening verse of the prologue! Does this make Job an inspired text? An implicit narrative anthropomorphism—or is it a theomorphism?—identifies God's words with the initial description of Job.

Despite the events suggested by the title of this essay, there is no literal encounter between Job and the adversary, *ha-satan*. Such encounters are only implied, after the adversary "went out from the presence of God" to inflict catastrophes on Job. But after his physical setbacks,

Job's encounters with the adversary are rigorously continued in debates with his false friends. Eliphaz, Bildad, and Zophar speak many wise words, yet they err when they accuse Job of wrongdoing. At first, we may find nothing to reproach in the sober speech of Eliphaz:

> If one attempts a word [*davar*] with you, will you be weary?
> But who can refrain from speaking?
> Behold, you have instructed many,
> And you have strengthened weak hands.
> Your words have upheld the stumbler,
> And you have encouraged feeble knees.
> But now it comes upon you, and you are weary,
> It touches you, and you are frightened.
> Is not your fear of God your confidence [*kislatecha*],
> And your hope the integrity of your ways?
> Remember, who that was innocent ever perished?
>
> (4:2–7)

Once again we encounter a series of questions. What is Eliphaz's mode of questioning? The first question appears as a gentle request; Elihu asks whether he may respond to Job. Yet he is not interested in Job's answer, for he cannot resist speaking. Eliphaz accuses Job of hypocrisy: "Your words have upheld the stumbler . . . / But now it comes upon you, and you are weary." Eliphaz further employs leading questions that do not aim at conversation, but only accuse Job: "Who that was innocent ever perished?" By implication, if Job perishes, he is guilty. We begin to see that Job's companions are his accusers, his adversaries.

If this seems unlikely, consider a remarkable passage in tractate Sanhedrin of the Babylonian Talmud. To modern readers, this Talmudic narrative may appear to be a fanciful reconstruction. But such legends often achieve significant interpretations. In a deliberately anachronistic commentary on the binding of Isaac (Gen. 22), the Rabbinic sources draw from the Book of Job. On this model, they first explain God's command that Abraham sacrifice his son:

> "After these things, God tested Abraham."
> After the words of *satan,* as it is written, "And the child grew, and was weaned" [Gen. 21:8]. *Satan* spoke before the Holy One, blessed be He: Master of the Universe! You graced this old man with the fruit of the womb at the age of

a hundred, yet of all the banquet he prepared, he did not have one turtle-dove or pigeon to sacrifice before You.

(Sanhedrin 89b)

The Rabbis interpret the test of Abraham as a parallel to Job's trials. But *satan* appears here without the definite article: *satan* is either a proper name, perhaps influenced by Persian, dualistic ideas, or refers to some indefinite adversary.

According to tradition, there is no early and late, and hence no time in Scripture; God's language is beyond time. Once Job has been alluded to, then, the cross-references multiply. To explain why Abraham's journey to Moriah lasts three days, the Rabbis describe several obstacles, including an encounter with *satan*.

Satan anticipated him on the way and said to him, "If one attempts a word [*davar*] with you, will you be weary? . . . Behold, you have instructed many, and you have strengthened weak hands. Your words have upheld the stumbler. . . . But now it has come upon you, and you are weary." [Job 4:2–5].

He [Abraham] said to him, "I will walk in my integrity" [Ps. 26:1].

He said to him, "Is not your fear of God your foolishness [*kislatecha*]?" [Job 4:6].

He said to him, "Remember, who that was innocent ever perished?" [Job 4:7].

(Sanhedrin 89b)

The absence of names produces a somewhat dizzying effect. We almost lose track of the speakers, as both the adversary and Abraham employ phrases from the Book of Job and the Psalms. In fact there are no speakers; there are only quotations from Scripture. At the same time, the retelling of Abraham's story sheds light on the story of Job. If *satan*—without the definite article—can speak like Eliphaz, then we have an insight into the character of Eliphaz as an adversary, a *satan*. Notice, in passing, that the adversary resorts to a deceptive play on words. Eliphaz asks, "Is not your fear of God your confidence?" But *satan* plays on a further meaning of *kislatecha,* and turns this verse into the aggressive challenge: "Is not your fear of God your foolishness?" Or perhaps this insidious hint is already present when Eliphaz speaks these words.

But the Rabbinic revision of Abraham and Job presses further. If Eliphaz has been identified with the adversary, Abraham is identified with Eliphaz, for he defends himself with the question Eliphaz raises: "Who that was innocent ever perished?" Eliphaz accuses Job with this question, while Abraham uses it in self-defense. What the companions say is not necessarily wrong, but they wrongly address themselves to the righteous Job. Depending on context, Eliphaz's words are appropriate to either *satan* or to Abraham. Context also determines whether a friend speaks as an adversary, or whether perhaps Job speaks as his own enemy. May we interpret the disputes between Job and his friends as reflections of an internal struggle? Abraham's encounters with the adversary might be viewed as encounters between reason and irrationality, between waking consciousness and the unconscious.

Before hastily accepting or rejecting a psychological interpretation, we should read further. How does the discussion between Job and his companions proceed? We can hardly refer to it as a "dialogue," for the speakers seldom respond to each other. What is the difference between Job's language and that of his friends?

Eliphaz, Bildad, and Zophar only strive to justify Job's suffering. They employ pseudo-questions, not in order to probe the mystery of God's justice, but to confront Job with conventional wisdom. A battle ensues between normative beliefs and personal experience. The friends attempt to force Job back to traditional ideas, but since Job denies that he is guilty, he wishes to question God directly:

> I will give free utterance to my complaint,
> I will speak in the bitterness of my soul.
> I will say to God: Do not condemn me,
> Let me know why you contend with me.
> Is it good for you to oppress,
> To despise the work of your hands,
> And shine upon the counsel of the wicked?
>
> (10:1–2)

The friends express platitudes, but Job seeks a more original and convincing form of language in debate with God. Casting aside their clichés, he says:

> What you know, I also know,
> I am not inferior to you.
> Yet, I shall speak to Shaddai,

> And I desire to reason with God.
>
> (13:2–3)

The debates evolve, or fail to evolve, in three cycles: Job 4–14, 15–21, and 22–31. As we move from the first to the second round, however, a change occurs. The false friends become more hostile, and Job finds he must respond to their attacks. They briefly succeed in deflecting him from his intention to address God, as he tries to defend against their slanders and commonplaces. There can be no clear resolution in such a dispute between orthodox thought and an individual who seeks immediate knowledge of God. The problem for Job is not to attain wisdom, which he already possesses, but to reconcile his knowledge with his suffering.

After the third cycle of speeches, which appears to have been distorted by scribal errors or tampered with by editors, we come to Elihu's tirade. This new voice may have been added at a later date, and combines polemic with subtler arguments. In a sense, Elihu acts as the first literary critic of the book, when in chapter 32 he complains that the other speakers have not answered Job. He, on the contrary, employs relatively accurate quotations in chapters 33 and 34, and attempts direct rebuttals. Further, Elihu introduces a new mode of questioning. The friends have raised *leading questions,* which imply that Job is guilty. Job asks *probing questions,* aimed toward truer dialogue and an individual grasp of God's ways. Now Elihu brings in a rhetorical style that involves borderline or *limit questions.* There are hints of this kind of questioning throughout the Wisdom literature, but it becomes decisive at the end of Elihu's speech:

> Stand still, and consider the wonders of God.
> Do you know how God commands them,
> And causes the lightning of His cloud?
> Do you know the balancings of the clouds,
> The wonders of one perfect in knowledge?
>
> . . . .
>
> Can you, with Him, spread out the sky,
> Which is strong as a molten mirror?
>
> (37:14–18)

These are questions that compel us to be silent, questions that can only be answered by God, if at all.

Behind what are called "rhetorical questions," then, we discern unexpected nuances. Many questions work only as accusations, others probe for an answer, while a few provoke an inspired dialogue. The sequence of questions builds toward dialogue with God. In the circle of friends, Elihu comes closest to dialogue, when he quotes and tries to refute Job's words. God's response cannot come until Job and his companions have exhausted themselves in efforts to achieve either dialogue or a stable theological position.

Yet as God answers Job out of the whirlwind, He essentially radicalizes the form of the limit question:

> Who is this that darkens counsel
> By words without knowledge?
>
> . . . .
>
> Where were you when I laid the foundations of the earth?
> Declare, if you have understanding.
> Who determined the measurements, if you know?
> Or who stretched the line upon it?
> Where are its foundations fastened?
>
> (38:4–6)

What is the quality of these questions? And how has the author of the text dared to represent God's speech? By raising this form of question, God asserts nothing, but only reveals the inadequacy of human assertions. A trope is a turn; when God answers Job, His questioning tropes on, or turns away from, all the assertions demanded of Him.

Only Job shows real understanding when he reiterates the question God has asked: "Who is it that darkens counsel / By words without knowledge?" Many interpreters conceive this as a leading question, addressed to Job, but it is more complex. After all, the companions are guiltier than Job of "darkening counsel." But only Job accepts the question as being addressed to him; only he appears capable of receiving God's words. Job combines an allusion to God's question with a genuine, self-abasing response:

> Who is this that hides counsel, without knowledge?
> Therefore I have uttered what I did not understand,
> Things too wonderful for me, which I did not know.
>
> (42:3)

At this moment, Job attains the I-Thou relationship to God he has sought. Surely he cannot expect solutions to the vast questions he has raised. The only answer is a sequence of questions that leads to the human recognition: I am nothing, I know nothing. Only God truly is, so that Hebrew employs the present tense of the verb, "to be," only in reference to God.

III

I conclude with several questions and hesitant answers. Who or what is *ha-satan,* the adversary? Depending on context, and even within a single passage, this key word may be interpreted on several levels. First, "the adversary" can be read as a metaphysical force of evil or reversal, fate or accident, or as an evil being that accuses men and women before God. But this literal reading of *ha-satan* comes dangerously close to positing a dualistic distinction between God and evil. Second, "the adversary" can be viewed as being embodied in false friends. Third, moving further from the *pshat* or literal level, "the adversary" may be a part of oneself, an enemy within, perhaps the irrational impulses of the id—or the tyrannical commonplaces of the superego. Finally, through rhetorical analyses which extend the conclusions of previous methods, "the adversary" may be understood to represent a form of misguided language. False questions and assertions oppose those who strive for a dialogical relationship to God. As *satan* is an aspect of God, rather than His antithesis, so misguided language forms part of language in general. *Satan* becomes associated with deceptive rhetoric, especially when it asserts too much, or raises misleading questions. To decide that encounters with the adversary are only encounters with language, with oneself, or with other human beings, would be a humanistic reduction. Instead, we should leave all four levels of meaning open.

In what sense does God answer Job? Not by offering information, but only by affirming the necessity of questions, rather than dogmatic assertions. What, then, is the final significance of the different forms of questioning employed by Job's companions, Job, and God? The false friends rely on theological dogmas and believe that they can explain the significance of Job's suffering. Job's inquisitive language, on the other hand, involves him in a project of "deconstructing theology," which shows itself as a more adequate, though also problematic, way to approach God.

Does this mean that the prologue and epilogue, by telling stories about God, contradict the negative wisdom suggested by the Book of Job? Job does indeed subvert the Wisdom literature of which he forms a part. One is tempted to say that the text undoes itself: by narrating a dialogue between God and "the sons of God," it contradicts the explicit argument against theological statements. Yet, just as *ha-satan* must not be read only literally, so the words of God must be read on several levels. Some readers are content to believe that God appears to Job and speaks with him. But the text does not tell us this; rather, God answers "out of the whirlwind." Most modern readers will be more comfortable with the notion that amid a sudden storm, Job senses God speaking to him, and raising questions about mysteries of creation.

Yet we should not be content to leave it at that. What is the essence of God's speech? Job learns, most profoundly, a way of approaching God through language and its annulment. Even if the friends have not recognized the errors of their words, Job learns a kind of linguistic asceticism that is one basic tendency in Jewish thought. He knows not to affirm what is beyond the limits of his understanding, and especially not to seek a clear perception of God. If the God that can be spoken of is not the eternal God, then how can theology presume to be a language of God? Jewish theology is at war within itself, constantly forced to reject its own positive statements. When God asks, "Who is it that darkens counsel / By words without knowledge?" Job turns the question toward himself and affirms silence:

> Behold, I am of small account;
> What shall I answer you?
> I place my hand upon my mouth.
>
> (40:4)

"The Ancient Trail Trodden by the Wicked": Job as Scapegoat

René Girard

What do we know about the Book of Job? Not very much. The protagonist bemoans his fate interminably. He has just lost his sons and all his cattle. He scratches his ulcers. The misfortunes which cause him to moan are duly enumerated in the prologue. It is the wickedness which Satan has just done to him, with God's permission.

So we think we know but do we really? Not once in the course of the dialogues does Job mention Satan nor anything about his wickedness. Many will say that all this is too present to his mind and to the mind of his friends so he doesn't have to allude to it.

Perhaps so, but there is something else altogether that Job does talk about, and more than just allusively. He does not remain silent about the cause of his misfortune; he insists strenuously. And it is none of the causes that the prologue talks about. It is a cause which is neither divine, nor Satanic, nor material but human, only human.

The strange thing is that across the centuries commentators have never taken that cause the least bit into account. Doubtless I do not know them all but those whom I do know pass over that cause in silence, systematically. It appears that they don't see it. Whether they are ancient or modern, atheist, Protestant, Catholic or Jew, they never ask themselves about the object of Job's complaints. The question appears resolved for them once and for all by the prologue. Everyone sticks religiously to the ulcers, the lost cattle, etc.

From *Semeia* 33 (1985). © 1985 by the Society of Biblical Literature. Translated by Andrew J. McKenna.

And yet, for some time, the exegetes have been warning their readers against this prologue. Its little story, we are told, is not up to the level of the dialogues. We must not take it too seriously. That is all very well, but unfortunately the exegetes do not always follow their own advice. They do not understand what it is in the dialogues that manifestly contradicts the prologue.

In order to contest the traditional vision of the work, do we absolutely have to know Hebrew, do we have to plunge ourselves into the numerous enigmas of this formidable text, do we have to emerge with ever more original solutions? Absolutely not. It is enough to read the translations. If scientific erudition were necessary, I would not allow myself to utter a word, because I am not a Hebraist. The novelty which I am proposing is not hidden in some obscure recess of the Book of Job. It is very explicit; it is spread out over numerous and lengthy passages which contain nothing ambiguous or obscure.

Job tells us clearly what he suffers from: he finds himself ostracized, persecuted by those around him. He hasn't done any evil, and everyone turns away from him, everyone has become very harsh towards him. He is the scapegoat of the community.

> My brothers stand aloof from me,
> and my relations take care to avoid me.
> My kindred and my friends have all gone away,
> and the guests in my house have forgotten me.
> Their serving maids look on me as a foreigner,
> a stranger, never seen before.
> My servant does not answer when I call him,
> and I am reduced to entreating him.
> To my wife my breath is unbearable,
> And for my own brothers I am a thing corrupt.
> Even the children look down on me,
> ever ready with a jibe when I appear.
> All my dearest friends recoil from me in horror:
> Those I loved best have turned against me.
>
> (19:13–19)

Job reminds us of the scapegoat down to that fetid odor which his wife reproaches him for spreading and which reappears, in significant ways, in a number of primitive myths.

We mustn't allow the allusion to a real goat arouse any misunderstanding. When I speak of the scapegoat, I am not thinking about the animal used in sacrifices, about the famous rite in Leviticus. I am using the expression in the sense in which we all use it without thinking, in connection with what happens around us in politics, in professional life, in family life. This usage is modern and of course does not show up in the Book of Job. But the phenomenon shows up, with something more savage. The scapegoat is the innocent person who polarizes universal hatred around him. That is exactly what Job is complaining about:

> And now ill will drives me to distraction,
> and a whole host molests me,
> rising, like some witness for the prosecution,
> to utter slander to my very face.
> In tearing fury it pursues me,
> with gnashing teeths.
> My enemies whet their eyes on me,
> and open gaping jaws.
> Their insults strike like slaps in the face
> and all set on me together.
>
> (16:7–10)

Revealing passages such as this are superabundant. As I cannot multiply quotations forever, I choose what seems to me a rather striking passage where the scapegoat is concerned. Chapter 30:1–12 brings into the picture a subgroup which in Job's society plays the role of permanent scapegoat.

> And now I am the laughing stock
> of my juniors, the young people,
> whose fathers I did not consider fit
> to put with the dogs that looked after my flock.
>
> . . . .
>
> That brood of theirs rises to right of me,
> stones are their weapons.
>
> (30:1,12)

Historians do not know if it is a question here of a racial or religious minority, or perhaps of a kind of sub-proletariat which is subjected to the same sort of regime as the lowest castes in India. It doesn't matter. These people do not interest the author in themselves; they are only there to allow Job to situate himself in relation to them, to define himself as the scapegoat of these scapegoats, the one who is persecuted by those very people who can least offer themselves the luxury of persecution: Job is the victim of all without exception, the goat of the goats and the victim of the victims.

Job complains of physical ills, certainly, but that particular complaint relates clearly to the fundamental source of his woe. He is the victim of innumerable brutalities; the psychological pressure which weighs down on him is not to be born. Job thinks that even his life is begrudged him, especially his life perhaps. He thinks that he is going to die a violent death: he imagines the shedding of his own blood:

> Cover not my blood, O earth,
> afford my cry no place to rest.
> (16:18)

Am I carried away by my desire to find everywhere my own theses? Here is the explanatory note of the Jerusalem Bible on these two verses: "Blood, if not covered with earth, cries to heaven to vengeance . . . Job, mortally wounded, wishes to leave behind a lasting appeal for vindication: on earth, his blood; with God, the sound of his prayer."

The translation of the two verses and the note are in complete conformity with what we find in the other great translations, the French ones as well as those in other languages. The language of the note remains ambiguous, of course. By whom is Job mortally wounded? It could be by God alone rather than by men, but it is certainly not against God that the blood of the victim cries out for vengeance; it cries out for vengeance before God, just like the blood of Abel, that first great victim exhumed by the Bible. Yahweh says to Cain: "What have you done? Listen to the sound of your brother's blood, crying out to me from the ground" (Gen. 4:10).

But against whom does the blood which has been shed cry out for vengeance, who could seek to smother Job's cry, to efface his words, in order to prevent them from reaching God? It is strange that these elementary and decisive questions are never asked.

Job comes back tirelessly to the role of the community in what is happening to him but, and here is the mystery, he no more succeeds in making himself heard by commentators outside the text than by his interlocutors in the book. . . . No one takes the least account of what he says.

The revelation of the scapegoat has as little existence for posterity as for his friends. And yet we wish to be very attentive to what Job says; we pity him for not being understood. But we are so concerned with making God responsible for man's misfortunes, especially if we don't believe in Him, that the final result remains the same. We are only a little more hypocritical than Job's friends. For all those who pretend that they have always been listening to Job but who basically have not been listening at all, his words are only wind. The only difference is that we no longer dare to proclaim our indifference, whereas Job's friends, for their part, still dare to do so:

> Is there no end to these words of yours,
> to your long-winded blustering?
>
> (8:2)

This role of victim which Job attributes to himself is necessarily significant within an ensemble of texts, the Bible, where victims always and everywhere appear in the forefront. It takes but a moment's reflection to realize that we must view from a common perspective, that of the victim surrounded by numerous enemies, the reason for the astonishing resemblance between Job's speeches and what we call the pentitential psalms.

On these tragic psalms, we must consult the book by Raymund Schwager, *Brauchen wir einen Sündenbock?* We find in these texts the situation that Job is complaining about in an extremely condensed form. It is an innocent victim who is speaking. He is always in a situation which we may describe as a lynching. As Schwager has clearly shown, a scapegoat in the modern sense is describing to us the cruelties which he is being subjected to. There is only one difference but it has great consequences. In the psalms, only the victim speaks. In the dialogues of Job, other voices make themselves heard.

To bring together, as I have done, the most revealing passages on Job as scapegoat is to bring together the texts which are most similar to these psalms, similar to the point of being frequently interchangeable. That is, finally, to put the accent on what, for lack of a better term, we are calling the surrogate victim, that formidable common denominator of many biblical texts which has been mysteriously neglected by everyone. It has been the object of an intellectual expulsion that we must not, I think, hesitate to regard as continuous with the physical violence of antiquity.

To counter the harmful influence of the prologue, and so to finally understand what is at issue in Job, a rereading of a few psalms is a very healthy exercise.

> To every one of my oppressors
> I am contemptible, [un scandale]
> loathsome to my neighbors,
> and to my friends a thing of fear.
>
> (31:11)

Why has Job become the bête noire of the community? No direct answer is given. Perhaps it is better that way. If the author gave us something too solid to chew on, if he mentioned any incident, a possible origin of any sort, we would immediately think we understood, we would stop asking questions. Actually we would know less than ever.

Let us not imagine, however, that the dialogues maintain an absolute silence. They are full of information, but we have to know where to look for it. On the choice of Job as scapegoat, you cannot just go and ask anyone. The "friends," for example, say nothing very interesting about this. They want to make Job responsible for the cruelties that he is subjected to. They suggest that his avarice has ruined him; perhaps he has shown himself to be harsh towards the people; he took advantage of his position to exploit the weak and the poor.

Job passes for virtuous but, just like Oedipus perhaps, he has succeeded in committing a quite invisible crime. If not he, his son then, or another member of his family. A man condemned by the voice of the public could not be innocent. But Job defends himself with vigor, though no accusation is withheld. The indictments do not hold up.

Job does not say that he has never sinned, he says that he has done nothing to deserve his extreme disgrace; just yesterday he was thought to be infallible, he was treated like a saint; today everyone condemns him. It is not he who has changed, it is the men around him. The Job whom everyone execrates cannot be very different than the Job whom everyone venerated.

The Job of the dialogues is not a vulgar nouveau riche who has lost all his money. He is not simply a particular individual who succeeded at first, then "had some problems" and decided to meditate with his friends on the attributes of God and the metaphysics of evil. The Job of the dialogues is not the Job of the prologue. He is a great leader whom public opinion once exalted then brusquely repudiated. Consider chapter 29:2–25, which closes:

If I smiled at them, it was too good to be true,
they watched my face for the least sign of favor.
In a lordly style, I told them which course to take,
and like a king amid his armies,
I lead them where I chose.

The contrast between the present and the past is not a contrast between wealth and poverty, between health and illness, it is a contrast between the favor and the disfavor of one and the same public. The dialogues are not dealing with a purely personal drama, with a human interest story, but with the behavior of all the people towards a sort of "statesman" whose career has been shattered.

As fanciful as they are, the accusations against Job are revealing. The fallen potentate is especially reproached for abuses of power, and of the sort that could not be the work of a simple landowner, however rich we may suppose him to be. Job makes us think rather of the *tyrant* of the Greek cities. Why, Eliphaz asks him, has Shaddai turned against you?

Would he punish you for your piety,
and haul you off to judgement?
No, rather for your manifold wickedness,
for your unending iniquities!
You have exacted needless pledges from your brothers,
and men go naked now through your despoiling;
you have grudged water to the thirsty man,
and refused bread to the hungry;
and you have narrowed the lands of the poor man down to
     nothing
to set your crony in his place,
sent widows away empty handed
and crushed the arms of orphans.

(22:4–9)

The modern reader gladly adopts the vision of the prologue because it reminds us of our world, or at least the idea that we make of it. Happiness consists in possessing most everything possible without ever falling sick, in an eternal frenzy of joyous consumerism. In the dialogues, on the other hand, the only thing that counts is the relation between Job and the community.

Job presents his triumphal period as the autumn of his life, that is to say: the season which precedes the glacial winter of persecution. It is probable that the disgrace is recent and that it was sudden. Up to the last moment, Job suspected nothing of the reversal which was being prepared:

> My praises echoed in every ear,
> and never an eye but smiled on me;
>
> (29:11)

The mystery of Job is presented in a context which does not explain it but which allows us all the better to situate it in causal terms. The scapegoat is a broken idol. The rise and fall of Job are bound up with each other; we have the feeling that these extremes touch each other. We cannot interpret them separately and yet we cannot say that the first is the cause of the second. We sense a social phenomenon which is poorly defined but quite real, a phenomenon whose unfolding is not certain but probable.

The only common point between the two periods is the unanimity of the community, first in its adoration, then in its detestation. Job is the victim of the massive and sudden reversal of a public opinion which is necessarily unstable, capricious, a stranger to any moderation. He hardly appears any more responsible for the change in this crowd than is Jesus for a very similar change, between Palm Sunday and the Passion of the following Friday.

In order for there to be unanimity in both directions, there must be a mimetic contagion at work in each case. The members of the community influence each other reciprocally, they imitate each other in their fanatical adulation and then in their still more fanatical hostility. We will return to this issue later on.

In the last of his three speeches, one of the three friends, Eliphaz of Teman, clearly alludes to Job's predecessors in the double career of all powerful upstart and of scapegoat:

> And will you still follow the ancient trail
> trodden by the wicked?
> Those men who were borne off before their time,
> with rivers swamping their foundations,
> because they said to God, "Go away,
> What could Shaddai do to us?"
> Yet he himself had filled their houses with good things,
> while these wicked men shut him out of their counsels.

At the sight of their ruin, good men rejoice,
and the innocent deride them:
"See how their greatness is brought to nothing!
See how their wealth has perished in the flames!"

(22:15–20)

The "ancient trail trodden by the wicked" begins with greatness, wealth, power, but it ends in a stunning disaster. These are the same two phases which we have just discovered in Job's adventure. It is exactly the same scenario.

As I myself have done, Eliphaz opposes and, as a consequence, makes a connection between the two phases. He sees that they form a whole and that we cannot interpret them separately. There is something about the rise of these men which prepares their downfall. Our basic intuition, in short, is found in these words by Eliphaz. Job has already covered a good part of the way on the "ancient trail trodden by the wicked." He is at the beginning of the last stage.

The events which Eliphaz evokes appear distant, therefore exceptional; but not so exceptional as to prevent the observer from seeing their connection with Job and recognizing in them a recurrent phenomenon. A whole route is quite laid out here: many men have already taken it and now it is Job's turn. All these tragic destinies have the characteristic traits of the broken idol. Their destiny, like Job's, is necessarily determined by the metamorphosis of an adoring crowd into a persecuting crowd.

Eliphaz would not be able to make allusions to events which he situates in the *past,* if the disasters affecting the "wicked" were imaginary. He must be evoking an experience known to all, because it is the experience of the entire community. The violent defeat of the "wicked" remains present in everyone's memory. This sort of affair impresses men too strongly to fall into oblivion. Its stereotyped character helps one to remember it.

It is the same story, it happens again and again, and the warning given by Eliphaz is very reasonable. This is a wise man. Job would do well to take stock of his words. But how can he do so without repudiating his very own self, without admitting that he is guilty.

Is it certain that the "wicked" men are all victims of popular violence? What else could it be a question of? Reread the last four verses of the quote. They allude to a kind of lynching:

At the sight of their ruin, good men rejoice
and the innocent deride them:
"See how their greatness is brought to nothing!
See how their wealth has perished in the flames!"

In the context of a village society, the rejoicing of "good men" and the mockery of the "innocent" cannot be without consequences. We have to reflect here on the formidable efficacity of unanimous reprobation in such a milieu. In order to bring about all the disasters that are ascribed to him, God has only to give a free hand to these good men who call upon the authority of His vengeance.

The disaster which awaits the "wicked" at the term of their career, at the end of the "ancient trail," probably resembles those primitive Feasts whose activities, however attenuated and ritualized, makes us think of a crowd phenomenon. Everything always ends with some form of scapegoat who is burned or drowned. In former times, ethnologists caught the scent of more extreme violence behind the ritual forms they observed. Many contemporary researchers regard them as victims of their romantic and colonialist imagination. I think on the contrary that they were right. To discover in the dialogues the kind of violence we have discovered there owes nothing to colonialism and constitutes, it seems to me, an argument in favor of their thesis.

Many other passages suggest that the central event of the work, the terrible adventure which has just begun for the hero, is a recurrent phenomenon of collective violence which especially strikes the "great," the "tyrants," but not them exclusively; it is always interpreted as divine vengeance, the punitive intervention of the divinity.

I will cite but one example of it here. It is part of the speech of Elihu, the fourth of Job's lecturers. According to general opinion this character does not belong to the original dialogues. He is probably the work of a reader who was scandalized by the impotence of the first three guardians of public order. Elihu scorns the entrenchment of the three in tradition. He presents himself as a man who is "up to date," as a "modern," and he is confident of succeeding where the three others have failed.

He thinks he is more capable simply because he is younger and because he despises the past. We are all quite familiar with this sort of hollow contestation. He doesn't get to the bottom of things. He too seeks to reduce Job to silence but he just repeats in a less savory style what the three others have already recited. He belongs to a stage in which the ancient tradition is more feeble. He nonetheless says things which render the hidden subject of the dialogues more obvious than ever.

The theme of Job as "oppressor of the people" already shows up with the three friends, but Elihu makes still greater use of it. Behind his politico-religious formulae, it is popular violence that shows through.

In an instant, God

> smashes great men's power without enquiry
> and sets up others in their places.
> He knows well enough what they are about,
> and one fine night he throws them down for me to trample on.
> He strikes men down for their wickedness,
> and makes them prisoners for all to see.
>
> (34:24–26)

I am quoting from the Jerusalem Bible: its translation suggests admirably the identity of the god and of the crowd. It is the god who overturns the great but it is the crowd which *tramples* on them. It is the god who puts the victims in chains, but his intervention is public. It is effected in the presence of that same crowd which has perhaps not remained completely passive before such an interesting spectacle. The great are broken "without enquiry," as we might have guessed. The crowd is always ready to lend a hand to the divinity when the latter decides to deal ruthlessly with the wicked. And right away other great people are found to replace those who have fallen. It is god himself who enthrones them, but it is the crowd who adores them, in order to discover a little later, of course, that they are a false elect, and that they are worth no more than their predecessors.

Vox populi, vox dei. As in Greek tragedy, the rise and fall of the great constitutes a *mystery* whose conclusion is what is most appreciated. Although it never changes, it is always impatiently awaited.

What do the three "friends" do with the scapegoat. The prologue tells us that they are there to "have pity" on Job and to "console" him. For all their verbosity, their speeches have nothing comforting about them. Critics have recognized this but they attribute the asperities of the friends to their clumsiness. They never really question the quality of these speakers as friends. They persist in believing that their intentions are good.

We don't look closely enough, I think, at what these alleged "friends" say. The first thing that strikes the reader who is not in any way predisposed towards them is the prodigious violence of their speech. Listen to Eliphaz:

> The life of the wicked is unceasing torment,
> the years allotted to the tyrant are numbered.
> The danger signal ever echoes in his ear,
> in the midst of peace the marauder swoops on him.
> He has no hope of fleeing from the darkness,
> but knows that he is destined for the sword,
> marked down as meat for the vulture.
>
> (15:20–23)

Passages of this kind are superabundant. There is always some wicked person, an oppressor of the people. He was all-powerful but he is no more so. God has cursed him. The vengeance of the celestial armies pursues him. One of the three friends, Cophar of Naamat (20:22–29) describes to us the destiny which awaits this mysterious tyrant in especially bloodthirsty terms: "On him God looses all his burning wrath, . . . An arsenal of terrors falls on him, / And all that is dark lies in ambush for him," etc.

The menacing tirades of Cophar find no justification from the perspective of the prologue. Why would a poor wretch, who is downtrodden by inexplicable accidents as Job passes for being, find himself being pursued on top of that by innumerable executioners of a mysterious "divine vengeance"? Why would someone who has just lost his health, his children, his fortune, arouse on top of that the formidable gathering of hostility which is described by the "friends"?

Could it be a question of someone else besides Job in these vociferations? Job is under no such illusion. On three occasions, at point blank, in the same military order, the three friends fire off their superb and sinister imprecations. Whom else could they be aimed at? Job is not yet completely that enemy of God who is always evoked in such language but that is what he could become; that is what he certainly will become if he persists in rebelling against the unanimous voice which condemns him.

That, in short, is the entire message of Eliphaz. The man who is called at times, "the enemy of God," at times the "accursed," or more simply "the wicked man," is one and the same as "the wicked" identified by Eliphaz in chapter 22. For this kind of black sheep there are five or six interchangeable labels. It is always the same threat which these speeches make to Job, that of collective violence, always more collective violence.

Job often has recourse to very realistic language in the passages concerning his experience as a victim; it is even crudely realistic, in conformity with the abasement which is his theme. In contrary fashion, the three friends adopt the style which is appropriate to the grandeur of their theme. Concrete details abound, to be sure, but everything is dressed up in the style of religious epic.

We have to distinguish therefore between two types of discourse, that of the friends and that of Job. We shall see later on that this distinction is not *always* valid but it certainly is for the passages which I have cited thus far. Between the complaints of the underdog and the epic style of the friends the distance is so great as to discourage at first any comparison between them. The celestial armies seem to have nothing in common with the petty persecutions that Job is complaining about.

But if Job and those friends of his were not speaking of the same thing, the dialogues would have no object, there would not properly speaking be dialogue. And that in fact is somewhat the impression of the reader who does not see the key role of the surrogate victim. The reader is struck by a certain incoherence affecting the text as a whole. The characters are not really speaking to one another. This is especially true of the friends. One might say they don't hear Job's complaints, Job's arguments.

Contemporary criticism concerns itself above all with the rhetorical differences between discourses. It takes less interest in what is being talked about than in the way it is talked about. The concern with what it blithely calls the referent is increasingly regarded as alien to literary phenomena, an attitude which is ultimately responsible for all the misunderstandings which poison our intelligence of great texts.

The exegetes of Job have never been able to discover the object which is common to the two types of discourse which we have just distinguished. But not until recently have they stopped looking for it, at least in theory. What characterizes contemporary criticism, on the other hand, is the temptation to abandon that search.

That must not happen. In the vituperations of the friends, the principle theme is the gigantic mobilization aroused by the god, decreed by him, organized by him, against his particular enemies, the enemies of this god. Innumerable hordes converge on the wretch.

Where do they come from? Why do powerful armies gather for the sole purpose of destroying an isolated adversary who is incapable of defending himself? Why such a waste of military power?

Let us recall the passages where Job describes his situation in the community. He is alone, surrounded by enemies. It is the same *all against one* that we find here but it is not the same style. Faced with the formidable celestial armies we do not think of Job's ignoble persecutors but it's the same numerical disproportion and it's the same enemy. We are dealing with one and the same phenomenon in both cases.

All these forces converge *simultaneously* on God's enemy. Plausibility is not always satisfied but the *all against one* of the scapegoat only stands out more clearly as a result. It is the only principle of organization but it controls everything. Whoever the adversaries may be, the relation of forces does not change. Behind the strangest, the most monstrous, the least human combatants, what always shows through is the gathering of modest villagers against a single adversary; this poor wretch whom they hold in their grasp is doubtless one of their own.

Consider the animals who fight for God: bulls, dogs, birds of prey, especially vultures. We find all these beasts in myths, and yet still more. They are of course the most ferocious; they are also the species which live in herds, and which hunt or charge collectively, or which feed together from corpses; they are the species which behave, or appear to behave, in the same way as men when they gather against a common adversary, when they go on a manhunt.

We always find allusions to the same fundamental motif, the destruction of a solitary victim by a host of enemies. It is the same violence in both cases. That is what we must examine to understand the relation of the two styles. Violence is the true "referent," which is poorly disguised in the threats of his friends, and not disguised at all in the words uttered by Job. As far apart as they appear from each other, these two kinds of discourse each deal in their own way with the same phenomenon: the hero's becoming a scapegoat, the lynching that Job feels is building up—towards him.

In sacred discourse, transcendence transfigures everything; we have the impression that everything is happening outside of human history. But we also have the contrary impression. Look at the victim sweat with anguish, look at the arrow going through his liver. This is the impression that Job's more realistic description makes on us. A cross check between the two kinds of discourse is easily made.

The host of enemies always derives from one and the same model, the human crowd. When divine vengeance is in the offing, there is nothing in the universe which does not begin to swirl, to turbulate in the sense of *turba,* the crowd, as illuminated by Michel Serres (*Hermes*), and woe betide the being around whom that irresistible turbulence gathers, woe betide the one who is swept up in it. The swirling pack is the mode of existence par excellence for divine vengeance. It throws itself on its victim and tears him to tiny pieces; the terrible appetite for violence is the same for all participants. None of them wishes to miss striking the decisive blow. The images of laceration and of fragmentation remind us of the innumerable dismemberments we find in mythology and ritual, of the innumerable variants of the Dionysiac *diasparagmos.*

The *all against one* of collective violence shows through even in the gathering of three, then of four, persons around Job, even in the structure of their discourses. The three, then the four, constitute a small crowd in the midst of a great crowd. The awkward reinforcement of Elihu underlines the structure of the botched kill which dominates the book from one end to the other.

Around the victim at bay, the innumerable troop of words gathers for the coup de grace. The three series of speeches resemble those flights of arrows aimed at the enemy of God. The hostile speeches are not merely an image of collective violence; they are a form of active participation. Job sees this clearly when he denounces the verbal laceration inflicted upon him. The three friends crush him with their speeches, they pulverize him with words (19:2).

Is it not an exaggeration to liken these words to a lynching? The friends do not indulge in gross insults or in physical brutality. They do not spit on Job. They belong to the elite. Do we not catch Job red-handed here in a flight of exaggeration, of "dramatization"? .

Absolutely not. By translating all the violence directed against Job as so much service rendered to God, these speeches justify past brutalities and they incite to new ones. They are more dreadful than the abuse heaped on him by the wretched. Their *performative* value is obvious.

The god of the friends always fights three against one, four against one, a thousand against one. He doesn't worry about chivalry, as no one fails to remark. But how pointless and antiquated is the irony which aims at the religious in the abstract, in toto, without ever wondering about what is behind these visions. For three centuries, everyone takes these visions to be simply imaginary. They are regarded as inventions which are inessential, which come after the invention of this god whose force resides in the number of combatants lined up beneath his banner.

It is believed that the metaphysical god is the fruit of a properly metaphysical imagination and that the celestial armies are secondary fabrications of relatively minor scope. I have always thought that we must reverse the direction of this genesis. We must begin with these armies, which are not at all celestial but which are nonetheless real. We must begin with collective violence. And, for once, we do not have to postulate that violence, to regard it as a simple hypothesis. The author holds it up before our eyes at every moment. It is one with that persecution that Job is complaining about and of which he is the victim.

The speeches of the friends reflect the sacred fury which takes hold of lynchers at the onset of the lynching. From Dionysiac *mania* to Polynesian *amok,* there are many diverse names to designate the collective trance which we also find in Greek tragedy. These inflamed tirades resemble those of the tragic choir in the moments preceding the destruction of the victim, the murder of Pentheus in *The Bacchae,* the discovery of the "culprit" in *Oedipus Rex.*

Before our very eyes the three friends sacralize violence with all their might. The insults and the petty brutalities are transformed into the grandiose accomplishments of a supernatural mission. All the participants become celestial warriors, the closest neighbors as well as the most distant, the respectable citizens as well as the tramps, the young as well as the old, even longtime friends, even the closest relative, even his old wife who says to Job: "curse God and die."

How can we deny the relevance of collective persecution in primitive religion for the understanding of these great texts in which we see the tireless alternation of the complaints of the persecuted victim with frenetic calls to murder, couched in the language of the sacred, a language which recalls that of the most savage rituals, the preparations for the collective dismemberment of the victim?

What the community reads automatically in every backfire against leaders elevated by popular favor is the intervention of absolute Justice. What is deployed in the speeches of the three friends is a veritable mythology of divine vengeance.

Because they participate in his lynching, the friends do not understand the role of scapegoat played by Job. The paradox of foundational violence is revealed here in spectacular fashion. Those who manufacture the sacred with their own violence are incapable of seeing the truth. That is just what makes the friends totally deaf to the appeals that Job makes unceasingly. The more they participate in the violence against the unfortunate wretch, the more they are carried away by their barbarous lyricism and the less they understand what they are doing.

The three friends know very well what the social order demands of them but this knowledge does not in any way contradict their fundamental ignorance concerning the scapegoat, their incapacity to conceive of Job's point of view. They have no suspicion of the moral reprobation which this phenomenon inspires in Job, and, beyond Job, in all of us, by the sole grace of the biblical text.

As the Gospels will later say of a similar affair, the three friends "know not what they do" on the moral and religious level. They know very well, on the other hand, what it is they have to do and not to do on the level of a certain victimary cuisine whose meaning tends to elude us though it is by no means beyond reach.

When we finally get to the true themes of the work and discover their coherence, we rediscover the "theory" proposed in *Violence and the Sacred* and the works which follow it.

What does that theory say? That the unanimous violence of the group is transfigured as an epiphany of the sacred. In *The Bacchae* the lynching of Pentheus is one with the epiphany of an avenging Dionysus. In the dialogues the lynching of Job and that of all the "wicked" is one with the intervention of divine vengeance.

In order for a human group to perceive its own violence as sacred, it must exercise that violence against a victim whose innocence leaves no trace—by the very fact of that unanimity. That is what I say in *Violence and the Sacred* and that is exactly what we have just seen.

Of the three friends, Bildad of Shuah appears to me as the one most prone to mythology. With him the theme of the celestial armies is building up to a mythology similar to that of the Greek Erynnies or of the German Walkyries. We see clearly here that the religion of Bildad and of his world has not much to do even with those manifestations of the biblical Yahweh which remain most contaminated by mythological violence.

> Disease devours his flesh (of the wicked)
> Death's First Born gnaws his limbs.
> He is torn from the shelter of his tent,
> and dragged before the King of Terrors.

The Lilith makes her home under his roof,
while people scatter brimstone on his holding.

(18:13–15)

I now read the note of the Jerusalem Bible:

The "King of Terrors," a figure from oriental and Greek
mythology (Nergal, Pluto, etc.), seems here to have infernal
spirits (Furies) at command to plague the wicked man even
during his lifetime. . . . Lilith, another figure of popular
legend, is a female demon. . . . Brimstone produces, or is
symbolic of, sterility and is possibly (in this passage) a
precaution against infection.

All the great mythological systems, and not only the Indo-European
ones, contain these bands of killers, male or female, who act together,
unanimously, and who, by so doing, produce the sacred, sometimes
even divinizing their victims. That is the fully mythological version of
the celestial armies, that is to say, Job's persecutors.

It is easy to criticize the activity of theorists from the outside and
in the abstract, but when we are dealing with the Book of Job the only
real choice, I am convinced, is between the old moralizing clichés on
the one hand, the problem of evil and its metaphysical aftermath
bequeathed to us by the prologue, and, on the other hand, the fearful
equivalence between violence and the sacred, an equivalence which is
not consciously affirmed by the friends, but which is consciously
repudiated by the scapegoat.

Far from imprisoning texts within any sort of interpretive yoke,
the thesis of the foundational victim allows them to reemerge from the
silence surrounding them. It frees them from the metaphysical and
moral trap which has been working so marvelously for millennia. The
interpreters fall into this trap all the more willingly because in so doing
they elude the double subversion of the received ideas, the religious
and antireligious ones alike, with which the attentive reader of the
dialogues is necessarily confronted.

An undertaking like mine can have no other goal than to "reduce"
a considerable mass of givens to a certain number of principles, as few
and as simple as possible. Far from being reprehensible, the quest for
universally valid principles appears to me to be alone worthy of pursuit.

It is often said that the victimary thesis is not truly demonstrable
because it is never directly legible in a text. It describes a structuring

process; it cannot be deduced directly from a single text. It is essentially comparative and hypothetical. I have said all of this myself. The reason is that, with respect to the victimary mechanism, all texts appear necessarily to belong to one or the other of the two following categories:

1. Myths whose structuring by the victimary mechanism cannot be directly shown: from the very fact that myths are structured by the victimary mechanism, the latter can nowhere appear. That is just what we observe once again in all the speeches which are not by Job. We cannot expect of the friends that they recognize their injustice. As with all those who make scapegoats, they take their victim to be guilty. For them, there isn't any scapegoat.

2. Texts in which this same mechanism appears in the light of day. The innocence of the victim is proclaimed; the scapegoat is manifest as such but the persecutors, for the same reason, are no longer around exulting in visions about divine vengeance and celestial armies. They are no longer there to reveal to us the structuring effect which the process exercises on their language, on their vision, on their behavior.

There is nothing more difficult than to detect the structuring mechanism which is at work in a text, to see it in action. It is rather like looking for depth on a two dimensional surface, the written text.

To the extent that that impossibility can be overcome, the dialogues overcome it. They are dialogues precisely in the sense that they present the two visions in counterpoint. The true revelations of the persecuted alternate with the lying and sacralized speeches of the persecutors.

Sometimes we do not even need this counterpoint. In certain statements I have quoted, those of Eliphaz, for example, on the "ancient trail trodden by the wicked," those of Elihu on the god who crushes the great "without enquiry" and on the crowd who tramples, the victimary process shows so clearly through the sacralization process that we no longer need to confront the two kinds of discourse.

But the Book of Job gives us so much more than that. What is most extraordinary, I find, is still the counterpoint of the two perspectives, which is made possible by the dialogue form; it is close to a theatrical mise-en-scène which would no longer have catharsis as its object but the disappearance of all catharsis.

We cannot take the correspondences between the two kinds of texts as mere coincidence. Even if he cannot speak in our own language, even if he is sometimes out of his depths and nonplussed by his own daring, the author manipulates these correspondences too powerfully to be unaware of them. The difference in perspective on one and the same collective violence constitutes the true subject of the dialogues. Opposed to the sacred lie of the friends is the true realism of Job.

There is an essential dimension of the victimary thesis that remains to be uncovered and that is mimesis. I think that all the conditions of its presence are found together here. Job's lost prestige must have been a personal acquisition. It does not seem that he could have owned it to some function that he performed, nor that it was inherited. Judging by the pleasure he drew from it, we sense that he did not always possess this prestige. This is a man promoted from the ranks.

In order to be as wildly praised and venerated as Job was before becoming a scapegoat, it doubtless sufficed in such a fickle society that initial success make of him the *primus inter pares*. The desires of the people of his class, that of the three "friends," Eliphaz of Teman, Bildad of Shuah and Cophar of Naamat, and still others, focused on that first difference and magnified it disproportionately. It is the elite, at first, who took Job as a model, who flattered him, venerated him, slavishly imitated him. The rest of the people followed, imitating the first imitators.

The absence of social distance favors the reciprocal imitation of equals. Job is identified with his success and to desire this success is to desire Job himself, to desire Job's incomparable being. This identification is eminently competitive, therefore ambivalent from the very start. In his own class, Job only has rivals who try to catch up to him. They all wish to become that sort of uncrowned king that he represents to them.

But royalty, by definition, is not shared. Job cannot succeed as he does without provoking formidable jealousy in his own milieu. He is the *model-obstacle* of the mimetic theory. He arouses Nietzschean resentment; admiration has a backwash, an undertow which never fails—this is the scandal!—to bruise the admirer on the barrier which the model becomes for him. From the very fact that it is based on mimetic desire, the fascination exercised by the rival who is too successful tends to turn into implacable hatred; it is always already mingled with that hatred. It is among people who are socially close that a kind of hateful fascination flourishes; that is the kind that shows through in almost every word of the "friends."

Job's friends evoke his past glory, as does Job himself, but not for the same reasons; they do it in order to lecture him, spitefully and ironically. They feast on the contrast between the present and the past. Their envy must have been powerful indeed to survive the discrediting of their idol. With somewhat obscene haste, they recall to Job the change in his fortune; they verify in a sense their own good fortune:

> If one should address a word to you, will you endure it?
> Yet who can keep silent?
> Many another, once, you schooled,
> giving strength to feeble hands;
> your words set right whoever wavered,
> and strengthened every failing knee.
> And now your turn has come, and you lose patience too;
> and it touches you, and you are overwhelmed.
>
> (4:2–5)

The envy of the "friends" and of the people of their milieu is essential to the passage from the first mimetic unanimity to the second. Equality of conditions sharpens the fundamental duplicity of mimetic reactions inspired by the "great man." The mimesis of envy and of hatred spreads as rapidly as the mimesis of admiration. It is the same mimesis which is transmuted once the model has become an obstacle, for mimesis is scandalized by that metamorphosis.

The spectacular downfall of Job in public opinion must have begun in Job's social circle and thereafter spread downwards. The untouchables of chapter 30 would never dare to attack Job as they do without encouragement from the upper class. This is scarcely a conjectural matter: the speeches of the friends are an incitement to popular violence.

There must exist therefore a certain interval between the reactions of the elite and those of the crowd. This interval allows us to interpret an important theme, which I have not yet developed, although it figures in the speech of Eliphaz on "the ancient trail trodden by the wicked." It is the theme of divine vengeance *delayed*.

Even when they are already the declared enemies of God, the wicked appear still laden with His blessings. Why this long mansuetude on the part of the divinity? The classic response offered by religious thinking which is victimary is that, far from being fooled, the god resorts to a strategy. He encourages on their part the arrogance which will some day prove fatal to them. The god delays his intervention in order to make the fall of the wicked as spectacular and as cruel as possible.

If we reject the sadistic conception of the divine which is implied by all this, we will have to interpret this idea of vengeance *delayed* in terms of the envious feelings which we sense among the friends of Job.

Job sees perfectly well that the scapegoat is interchangeable with those who persecute him with the greatest ferocity, the so-called friends. He imagines this reversal of the situation, in order to show that the only true difference is in the suffering he undergoes:

> I too could talk like you,
> were your soul in the plight of mine,
> I too could overwhelm you with sermons,
> I could shake my head over you,
> and speak words of encouragement,
> until my lips grew tired.
> But, while I am speaking, my suffering remains:
> (16:4–6)

Great men are too popular to succumb all at once to plots that proliferate around them. Mimetic jealousy smoulders for a long time in the shade. That, I think, is what is signified by the "delay" of divine vengeance. But opinion tires of idols; it ends up by burning what it once adored, having forgotten its own adoration. That is the triumph of the "friends" and that is the moment at which the dialogues are situated.

My reasoning retains a conjectural character inasmuch as the envy concerning Job is not explicit. The friends themselves say nothing about it, of course. Job only makes allusions to it. The text which would tie mimetic envy directly to the phenomenon of the sacralized scapegoat is not to be found in the Book of Job. But we do find it elsewhere in the Bible, in Psalm 73, which is at once very like and very unlike those from which I have already quoted; it is very similar in its subject and very different in its perspective.

The narrator presents himself as one of the Righteous, one faithful to the true God, and long discouraged by the apparent inertia of divine Justice. He insists explicitly on the envy inspired by the too brilliant career of those whom he presents, of course, as impious. Fortunately, God has finally decided to intervene.

Contrary to the other tragic psalms, which are all written from the point of view of the victim, this is one of the very rare psalms which reflects the other perspective, that of the friends. In fact it is the only one of which we can say without hesitation that it reflects the perspective of the persecutors:

> My feet were on the point of stumbling,
> a little further and I should have slipped,
> envying the arrogant as I did,
> and watching the wicked get rich.

What he took for the inertia of the god was a canny temporization:

> This is why my people turn to them
> and lap up all they say,
>
> . . . .
>
> until the day I pierced the mystery
> and saw the end in store for them;
> they are on a slippery slope, you put them there,
> you urge them on to ruin,
> untill suddenly they fall,
> done for, terrified to death.

The individual who is speaking to us has long been chomping at the bit before a man, or a group of men, who have long been popular but whose noisy success has abruptly ended in their "fall," in their being "terrified to death." It is the "ancient trail" once again. The people in question here have followed it up to the final precipice and if there existed a list of the "wicked," their names would be found on it next to that of Job.

In short, the narrator is the approving accomplice of a collective violence which he takes for divine. He allows us to imagine the intimate reflections of Job's enemies, those reflections which the three friends keep to themselves.

For proof that the essential here is the infatuation of the people, we have the sentence: "The people turn to them." From the viewpoint of the narrator, the people assure the success of those who ought not to succeed but who nonetheless do so and whose abuses of power last as long as their enjoyment of popular favor.

The Righteous one can very well identify the still moderate envy of his positive imitation; but let that envy become more intense, as a consequence of the obstacle, of the scandal, of the triumph of the "wicked," and it will turn to hatred; now the Righteous one no longer recognizes it. And yet if there is an envy worthy of the name, that is certainly it. The Righteous one interprets his counter-imitation, his most intense resentment, as foreign to envy, whereas it is the paroxysm of envy. What he sees is the epitome of right sentiments, he sees religious fervor in its purest state. There remains but a certain element of mystification, but it is capital—whereby he resembles the friends whose exceeding envy is transformed into religious hysteria.

Psalm 73 does not follow biblical inspiration at its highest register, where what we hear is the voice of the victim. It is very close to the inspiration of the friends in the Book of Job. The highest register of inspiration is that of Job, which alone is specifically biblical; it has no equivalent in the Greek world or anywhere else.

Psalm 73 nonetheless has its place in the ensemble constituted by the psalms dealing with the collective victim. We can see this quite well if we compare its role to the role of Job's interlocutors. If the Bible were simply to transfer the monopoly of speech from the persecutors to the victims, if it substituted a "slave morality" for a "master morality," as Nietzsche claims, the revelation would not be as powerful as it is, neither on the moral nor on the intellectual level, which in fact are one and the same level. We would not be called upon to confront perpetually the two perspectives. The Bible would only amount to the revenge, symbolic or real, to which Nietzsche reduces the biblical process. It would boil down to a process of mimetic doubles, an inversion of signs having no essential signification. It is, as we see, something altogether else.

Like Greek tragedy, the Prophets, the dialogues of Job and the psalms visibly reflect great crises; they are political and social crises to be sure, but they are also religious, and they are one with the decadence of sacrificial systems which are still functioning in the two societies. We find ourselves at a junction between a religious phenomenon which is still sacrificial in the strict sense and a political phenomenon which is *sacrificial* in the broad sense. On certain points it is already possible to translate the religious discourse into political discourse and vice versa. Thanks to the work of the people in CREA (Centre de recherches anthropologiques et épistémologiques) and still others, these possibilities are rapidly growing, but their development is going to be so upsetting for the social sciences that we can expect strong resistance to it.

In the dialogues, the conditions which I have shown to be favorable to all mimetic phenomena are visibly found together. The combination of imitation that is positive at first, then "negative," this combination of imitative resentment spread by the friends and by people of their kind is what clearly accounts for the two successive unanimities and for the order of their succession. This double mimesis is revealed in the splendid metaphor of the torrent.

My brothers have been fickle as a torrent,
as the course of a seasonal stream.
Ice is the food of their dark waters,
they well with the thawing of the snow;
but in the hot season they dry up,
with summer's heat they vanish.
Caravans leave the trail to find them,
go deep into the desert, and are lost.
The caravans of Tema look to them,
and on them Sheba's convoys build their hopes.
Their trust proves vain,
they reach them only to be thwarted.

(6:15–20)

Job says "my brothers have been fickle as a torrent." To whom, precisely, does the metaphor apply? If the word "brothers" only designates the three friends, Job's direct interlocutors, the metaphor would not be relevant. It must apply to the entire community which is hardly to be distinguished from the friends. Today it rains and friends are drops of water among other drops of water. If the sun shines tomorrow, we shall see them again—as grains of sand in the burning desert. . . .

The two unanimities which make of Job an idol and a scapegoat in turn correspond to the springtime flood and to the absolute drought which succeeds it. If the three friends were not always "plugged in" to the fashion of the moment, like everyone else, there would be no unanimity. Their mimesis makes them perfectly *representative* of a community which is itself mimetic. If all the citizens were present in person around Job, we would learn nothing that we do not already know. The three comrades suffice for all, just like the choir in Greek tragedy.

Let us look carefully at the metaphor of the torrent. It expresses not only the absence of what is most desirable, whatever that may be, but also the presence, overabundant, stifling, of what is undesirable, whatever that may be as well. This accursed stream always ends up by bringing the thing it holds back from us and which it makes us desire, but precisely when it brings us that thing, we don't desire it any more; indeed, we flee it like the plague and that very thing is the plague from now on.

What is diabolical about the torrent is its cyclical nature, the way it always finally keeps its promise, but always too late, to provide men with what it holds back from them all year round. As it periodically reverses what it gives and refuses, it always revives desires which it never satisfies. The waters which the caravans need badly were so abundant the day before as to render inconceivable their complete disappearance at the precise instant that this need arises.

Without any breaks in its articulation, the metaphor draws from the torrent alone the behavior of normal desire and that of a desire which is ultimately deadly. It dismisses with elegance and simplicity the false common sense which demands at least two causes to account for effects which appear to be so contrary, the duality, for example, of a "pleasure principle" and of a "death instinct." A single principle suffices for everything. Such is mimetic desire.

Those who rightly apprehend desire are so alarmed that they attribute it to the hostile machinations of a devil. The demon has but one goal, it appears, and that is to harm humanity. The Satan of the prologue plays the role that is played by God according to the three friends; it is the role of the torrent in Job's metaphor; it is ever the role of the community in the thrall of mimesis.

Desire takes its projections for reality. The image of the torrent describes the world not as it is at first but as it appears to men when their desire is exasperated, when the prohibitions crumble which protected them from implacable rivalries.

Immense regions of the planet have been transformed into deserts, it appears, because of the uses that men have made of it, because of their desire. The more the desert spreads, inside and outside us, the more we are tempted to blame reality, or God himself, or, worse still, our neighbor, the first Job who comes along. . . .

By focussing all at once all antagonism on one and the same adversary, the scapegoat causes all other conflicts to disappear, and when he disappears, so do all conflicts without exception, at least temporarily. He reestablishes peace in a way that appears properly miraculous, that reinforces a suddenly restored unity, and that presents itself as the intervention of some supernatural power, of a divinity.

This is a crucial point of the theory. The psychological, moral and social *efficacity* of the scapegoat is one with its religious function for it is this efficacity that makes of the scapegoat mechanism the source par excellence of all social transcendence. It is Job himself who defines his efficacity as a scapegoat, and in a way that is far superior to what we have been able to observe among ourselves. But it is certainly in order to weaken rather than to reinforce the system that the victim speaks of it; he does not speak to celebrate its merits, to provide it with any moral guarantee, to boast its advantages or to advise it as a method of government.

That is what the persecutors do, without even realizing it. Those who use scapegoats do not speak about them. These days, of course, they do speak of them; but they only speak of their own scapegoats in order to view them as something quite the opposite:

> I have become a byword among the people,
> and a creature on whose face to spit.
> My eyes grow dim with grief,
> and my limbs wear away like a shadow.
> At this honest men are shocked,
> and the guiltless man rails against the godless;
> just men grow more settled in their ways,
> those whose hands are clean add strength to strength.
>
> (17:6–9)

If our translation is correct, what Job is describing here is the beneficial effect on his own community that is produced by unjust persecution. I know of no other text where that effect stands out so boldly. It is the same thing as the *tragic effect,* the Aristotelian catharsis; but we are not dealing here with a theatrical representation, and Job does not try to embellish the truth of the operation with aesthetic flourishes.

The translation of this passage is not the same everywhere. The one I have chosen is, as usual, from the Jerusalem Bible, which I recognize as being particularly favorable to my thesis, and as being singularly different from many others. For many ancient and modern translators alike, the second part of this text says some vague things which tend to reverse its meaning. In the New English Bible this reversal is realized maximally and here is the result:

> Honest men are bewildered at this
> and the innocent are indignant at my plight.
> In spite of all, the righteous man maintains his course
> And he whose hands are clean grows strong again.

The man whose hands are clean adds strength to strength here not *because* but *in spite* of the unjust persecution. This interpretation appears to me to be erroneous in view of the context. What the English

Bible wants Job to be saying is contradicted by all the texts which we have read. If Job still enjoyed the esteem of the pure and the virtuous, he would not be abandoned by all without exception, he would not be the scapegoat which he describes in so many texts which everyone translates in the same way.

The Book of Job goes so far in its revelation of the scapegoat as the foundation of the sacred, of ethics, of aesthetics and of culture in general that I am not surprised to find such startling formulations as we have just read. If the Jerusalem Bible is right, the other translations bear witness to the resistance which our minds oppose to this revelation.

The Jerusalem Bible translates the second verse of this passage as "a creature on whose face to spit." According to Etienne Dhorme (Old Testament: Pléiade edition), a literal translation would give us: "I will be a public Tophet." Dhorme points out in a note that, for the commentator Ibn Ezar, the word Tophet is made up of two terms:

> the valley of Taphet, a place of shame according to Jeremiah, since it is where the Judeans practiced human sacrifice; their sons and daughters were offered up in flames. Taphet may also signify altar or hearth. The Jews read this word with the vowels of the word *boshet* which means shame.

Telescope the two terms, combine the vowels of the first and the consonants of the second and you get *Tophet*. The *public Tophet,* in the form of a man here, is the object of unanimous execration. That is to say: a scapegoat; I do not see any difference from one language to the other. There is no possible ambiguity. In spite of all the innumerable tricks that language plays on us, I see no reason to moan about its impotence to communicate unambiguous meaning.

Only the real efficacity of the surrogate process can explain the existence of ritual behavior. Amazed by this process, its participants try to reproduce it by imitating it scrupulously. A new victim becomes necessary since the preceding one is no longer around. The principle of substitution is implicit in the observations made by Eliphaz. If Job shows any wickedness, any perversity, he will become the substitute for "the wicked" who preceded him, and he will not be spared his itinerary on "the ancient trail."

Job is the substitute of the wicked men who preceded him. He must therefore be wicked in the same way and that is what everyone is trying to show. The effort is made all the more strenuous by Job who struggles against it like the very devil. He throws every sort of wrench into the sacrificial works but to no avail; for the demonstration of his guilt is secondary with respect to the spontaneous choice of the community.

Society has a good thing, an efficacious purge of its bad humours. It is therefore natural to try to regularize it, to stabilize it in a way that is most advantageous for everyone. That rational and prudent conduct is what inspires ritual. It is the metamorphosis of the surrogate mechanism into a periodic rite.

In certain of its aspects, the phenomenon which concerns us in the dialogues is already ritualized. Everything suggests that the friends are hardly improvising in their behavior towards Job but that they are resorting instead to well tried formulas. They have to conform to some kind of model. Their speeches give off a strong scent of sacrificial liturgy.

The quite rhythmic clamor of the three series of speeches reminds us of the tragic choir, and, beyond that, of the ritual recitations which in preparation for sacrifice are intended to excite the participants against the victim. By their incantatory, repetitive character, these vociferations mime the movement and the cries of a crowd which is polarized around a victim.

The victim is already designated; what must be done now is to focus on the scapegoat all the stray violence that is so dangerous to the community. That is what the three friends are doing with Job. They don't travel "the ancient trail of the wicked" themselves, thank god, but they control the traffic. They know all its detours. They exercise a properly ritual function, just like the choir in Greek tragedy. They assure the proper functioning of the victimary mechanism.

We can count on Job to make that sacrificial recipe explicit. The recalcitrant scapegoat has some observations of incomparable force. Rare, unfortunately, are the readers who are capable of appreciating their soundness. Job resorts to a strange metaphor, one that is unintelligible for all the disciplines which persist in their blindness about the true nature of sacrifice:

> Soon you will be casting lots for an orphan,
> and selling your friend at bargain prices!
>
> (6:27)

Job compares himself explicitly to the ideal victim, who has neither relatives, nor servants, nor neighbors, nor even a friend to defend him. He can be chosen without fear of reviving the divisions which sacrifice is intended to cure. In short, Job restates in sacrificial terms everything else we have heard him say. He is abandoned by all; a void opens up around him. His alleged friends make the situation worse by their suggestion that he is the latest edition of the "wicked," of the "enemies of God."

The tone adopted by Job is somberly ironic. If his remark has any weight, it is because we are in the context of a world in which human sacrifice is officially abolished, religiously discredited, but not so completely forgotten that the allusion to the orphan drawn by lot ceases to be intelligible. Perhaps the immolation of children is still practiced secretly in some reactionary quarters.

For many specialists, the understanding of sacrifice consists in properly determining the classifications of the particular system in question. They regard any theory as false, a priori, if it is based on distinctions or comparisons which do not figure in the language of that system.

To argue as I do that the matrix of all sacrifice is the collective process of victimization, the scapegoat in the ordinary sense, strikes some people as unjustifiable. The thesis shortcircuits distinctions which the liturgical systems never abolish. It is therefore easy to maintain that I do not respect the facts.

But fortunately for me, here is Job who does the same thing. He too indulges in unseemly comparisons. His metaphors constantly compare things which theoreticians who are respectful of the institutional letter never allow themselves to compare.

We can of course turn a deaf ear, we can always follow the example of the "friends," while modernizing their arguments. The Book of Job belongs indubitably to "literature," and the orphan drawn by lot is only a metaphor. I agree, but are we so convinced that nothing true is ever to be learned from literature and its metaphors? Is that metaphor of the orphan drawn by lots really incongruous, or is it on the contrary very well placed and perfectly justified? Is it one of those ultra-modern metaphors which aims at comparing two radically different things only for the sake of the gratuitous shock effect it produces, or is it a metaphor which juxtaposes two things whose comparison is otherwise surprising: not because of the intrinsic distance between two things but because on the contrary their extreme proximity had eluded us up to that point? Is it perhaps a metaphor which, if we permit it, could teach us things which it knows and which we do not?

I choose the second solution. The apparent neutrality of nonliterary sources is less rich and, in the final analysis, less trustworthy than great literature. Job is far better situated than we are to make sense out of sacrifice. His metaphors are only meaningful in terms of the generative link between collective persecution and ritualized sacrifice which I have proposed in *Violence and the Sacred*. The existence or nonexistence of this link cannot be made to depend upon whether such indications are given or not given by the systems of liturgical codification. It is quite obvious that these systems never trumpet their own entrenchment in violence. To give the last word to their explicit testimony where a theory of sacrifice is concerned is about as sensible as asking Job's community if the violence committed against him is real and as arbitrarily cruel as he claims it is.

Must we deny the status of victim to Job under the pretext that he is the only one to point it out to us and that neither the three friends nor anyone else in the community acknowledges him as a victim?

In a sense that is what is denied him by all the traditional interpretations. The most efficacious objections are never the most explicit ones. We gladly recognize in Job the victim of God, of the devil, of bad luck, of destiny, of "the human condition," of clericalism and anything else you wish, as long as it is never a question of Job's neighbor, that is to say, of ourselves.

What is this refusal to recognize the victim as such, what is this eternal claim of innocence on the part of humanity, if it is not the incomprehension which the dialogues have as their object to reveal? Secretly we always agree with the three friends who make a show, though not much of one, of pity for Job, but who treat him as guilty; they do this not only to make him their scapegoat but also to deny that such a thing is possible. The two always go together.

What Job says will always elude a mind which is bent on making classifications, whether it is structuralist or not. For this bent itself is the direct descendant of forms of intellectual discrimination which originate in the victimary mechanism and it will never break completely with it.

True anthropological knowledge cannot limit itself to reusing classifications which belong to the systems under study. It must account for them in a theory which is genetic and structural at once. Not any more than Job himself does the victimary theory grossly confuse spontaneous persecution with ritual sacrifice, but it does allow us to determine a relationship between spontaneous persecution and all sacrifice, a relationship which is both metaphorical and real: it is metaphorical in that all ritual activity consists in the substitution of a victim; it is real in that the substituted victim is nonetheless immolated.

Behind the apparent incoherence of the themes, a higher coherence is revealed, but only on one condition. We must interpret the difference in perspective to Job's benefit. We must prefer Job's discourse to what the others say: we must take the revelation of the scapegoat seriously. In a word, we must take it as being *true*.

It is in the light of what Job says that we can interpret the speeches of the friends as well as the whole of the dialogues, but we cannot do the reverse. What the friends say sheds absolutely no light on what Job says. There are two truths in the relative sense, in the sense of a "relativism" or a "perspectivism," but there is only one where knowledge is concerned, and that is the truth of the victim.

It is not enough for us to recognize the object of the debate, the collective violence which is preparing to descend on Job and which has already singed him; we must recognize the two perspectives on that violence and above all we must choose between them. Any avoidance of taking sides is a deception. Any affectation of *impassivity,* whatever its pretext, stoical, philosophical or scientific, perpetuates the status quo, prolongs the occultation of the scapegoat, and effectively makes us accomplice to the persecutors. Job is the opposite of that impassivity. Far from being a source of ignorance, the passionate identification with the victim is the only authentic source of knowledge as of everything else. The true science of man is not impassive.

Chronology

TEXTUAL

The E Source (ca. 850–800)

Amos, Proverbs 10–22:16 (ca. 750)
Hosea (ca. 725)
Micah, Proverbs 25–29, Isaiah 1–31, JE redaction (ca. 700)
Deuteronomy, Zephaniah (ca. 650)
Nahum, Proverbs 22: 17–24 (ca. 625)
Deuteronomy–Kings (ca. 600–500), Jeremiah, Habakkuk (ca. 600)
Job 3–31, 38–42:6 (ca. 575)
Isaiah 40–55, Job 32–37 (ca. 550)
Isaiah 56–66, Jeremiah 46–52, Ezekiel 1–37, 40–48, Lamentations (ca. 525)
Job redaction, the P Source, Haggai, Zechariah 1–8, Jeremiah 30–31 (ca. 500)
Additions to Ezekiel 1–37, 40–48 (ca. 475–400)
Joel, Malachi, Proverbs 30–31, Lists (ca. 450)
JEP redaction [Genesis–Numbers], Isaiah 32–35, Proverbs 1–9, Ruth, Obad (ca. 425)
JEPD redaction, Jonah, Psalms, Proverbs redaction Song of Songs, Chronicles, Ezra, Nehemiah (ca. 400)
Ecclesiastes (ca. 350)
Zechariah 9–14 (ca. 325)

HISTORICAL

900 B.C.E.

800 B.C.E.

The Fall of Samaria (ca. 720)
The Reformation of Josiah (ca. 700–600)

700 B.C.E.

The Fall of Jerusalem and the Exile to Babylonia (ca. 587–538)

600 B.C.E.

The Return (ca. 538)

500 B.C.E.

Nehemiah and Ezra (ca. 475–350)

400 B.C.E.

The Hellenistic Period (ca. 330–63)

TEXTUAL		HISTORICAL
Isaiah 24–27, Ezekiel 38–39 (ca. 300) The Septuagint, a translation of the Hebrew Bible into Greek (ca. 250–100)	300 B.C.E.	
	200 B.C.E.	The Maccabean Revolt (ca. 165)
Daniel (ca. 175) Esther (ca. 100)	100 B.C.E.	Pompey takes Jerusalem (ca. 63)
	10 B.C.E.	Birth of Christ (ca. 6)
	B.C.E. —— C.E.	
	10 C.E. 20 C.E.	
	30 C.E.	Baptism of Christ and the beginning of John's Ministry (ca. 26) Crucifixion of Christ and Pentecost (ca. 30) Conversion of Paul (ca. 32)
	40 C.E.	Martyrdom of James (ca. 44) Paul and Barnabas visit Jerusalem during famine (ca. 46)
Galatians (ca. 49) Thessalonian Letters (ca. 50)	50 C.E.	Paul's First Missionary Journey (ca. 47–48) Paul's Second Missionary Journey (ca. 49–52)

TEXTUAL		HISTORICAL
Corinthian Letters (ca. 53–55)	50 C.E.	Paul's Third Missionary Journey (ca. 52–56)
Romans (ca. 56)		Paul is arrested in Jerusalem and is imprisoned by Caesar (ca. 56–58)
		Paul's voyage to Rome and shipwreck (ca. 58)
Philippians (ca. 60)	60 C.E.	First Roman imprisonment of Paul (ca. 59–60)
Colossians, Philemon (ca. 61–62)		Paul's release and last travels (ca. 61–63)
Mark (65–67)		Paul's second Roman imprisonment, martyrdom and death (ca. 64–65)
		Death of Peter (ca. 64–65)
Matthew (75–80)	70 C.E.	Fall of Jerusalem (ca. 70)
	80 C.E.	
Canonization of the Hebrew Bible at Synod of Jammia (ca. 90)	90 C.E.	Persecutions under Emperor Domitian discussed in Revelation (ca. 93–96)
Ephesians, Hebrews, Revelation, Luke, Acts (ca. 95); 1 Peter (ca. 95–100), Fourth Gospel (ca. 95–115)		
Johannine Epistles (ca. 110–15)	100 C.E.	
James, Jude (ca. 125–50)	125 C.E.	
2 Peter (ca. 150)	150 C.E.	
Timothy, Titus (ca. 160–75)		

TEXTUAL

Date	Textual
175 C.E.	
200 C.E.	
300 C.E.	Stabilization of the New Testament canon of twenty-seven books (ca. 350–400)
400 C.E.	Jerome completes the Latin Vulgate, a translation of the Bible based on the Septuagint and translated from the Hebrew (ca. 400)
500 C.E.	
600 C.E.	
700 C.E.	
800 C.E.	
900 C.E.	
1000 C.E.	
1100 C.E.	
1200 C.E.	
1300 C.E.	The first translation of the Bible into English, by John Wycliffe (ca. 1382)
C.E. 1400	The Gutenburg Bible is printed from movable type, ushering in the new era of printing (1456)
1500 C.E.	Erasmus finishes a translation of the Bible into Greek (1516)

TEXTUAL

1500 C.E.

Martin Luther translates the Bible into German (1522)
William Tyndale and Miles Coverdale's English translations of the Bible (1535)
Matthew's Bible is produced, based on the Tyndale and Coverdale versions (1537)
The Great Bible is produced by Coverdale (1539)

1600 C.E.

The Geneva Bible, the first to separate chapters into verses (1560)
The Douay-Rheims Bible, a Catholic translation from Latin into English (1582–1610)
The King James Version is completed (1611)

1700 C.E.
1800 C.E.

1900 C.E.

The English Revised Version is coissued by English and American scholars (1885)
The American Standard Version (1901)
The Moffatt Bible (1924)
The Smith-Goodspeed Bible (1931)
The Confraternity Version, an Episcopal revision of the Douay-Rheims Bible (1941)
Knox's Version, based on the Latin Vulgate and authorized by the Catholic Church (1945–49)
The Revised Standard Version (1952)

TEXTUAL

The New English Bible, Protestant (1961)
The Jerusalem Bible, Catholic (1966)
The Modern Language Bible (1969)
The New American Bible, Catholic (1970)
Today's English Version (1976)
The New International Version (1978)
The New Jewish Version (1982)

1900 C.E.

Contributors

HAROLD BLOOM, Sterling Professor of the Humanities at Yale University, is the author of *The Anxiety of Influence, Poetry and Repression,* and many other volumes of literary criticism. His forthcoming study, *Freud: Transference and Authority,* attempts a full-scale reading of all of Freud's major writings. A MacArthur Prize Fellow, he is general editor of five series of literary criticism published by Chelsea House. During 1987–88, he served as Charles Eliot Norton Professor of Poetry at Harvard University.

PAUL RICOEUR is Professor Emeritus of Philosophy at the University of Paris (Nanterre) and the University of Chicago. Among his many works are *The Conflict of Interpretations: Essays on Hermeneutics, The Rule of Metaphor, The Symbolism of Evil, Interpretation Theory: Discourse and the Surplus of Meaning,* and *Time and Narrative.*

NORTHROP FRYE is University Professor Emeritus at the University of Toronto and one of the major literary critics in the Western tradition. His major works are *The Anatomy of Criticism, The Critical Path: An Essay on the Social Context of Literary Criticism,* and *Fearful Symmetry: A Study of William Blake.*

DAVID DAICHES is Regius Professor of English, Emeritus, at the University of Edinburgh. He is the author of *Critical Approaches to Literature, Literature and Society,* and *A Critical History of English Literature.*

ROBERT ALTER is Professor of Hebrew and Comparative Literature at the University of California at Berkeley. His books include *The Art of Biblical Narrative* and *Motives for Fiction.*

KEN FRIEDEN is Assistant Professor of Comparative Literature and Jewish Studies at Emory University. He is the author of *Genius and Monologue* and of a forthcoming study on dream interpretation.

143

René Girard is Andrew B. Hammond Professor of French Language and Literature at Stanford University. He is the author of *Deceit, Desire, and the Novel*, *Violence and the Sacred*, *To Double Business Bound*, and *The Scapegoat*.

Bibliography

Adar, Zvi. "The Book of Job." In *Humanistic Values in the Bible*, 397–418. New York: Reconstructionist Press, 1967.

Aizenberg, Edna. "Borges and the Book of Job." *Kentucky Romance Quarterly* 31 (1984): 89–96.

Anderson, Bernhard W. "The Beginning of Wisdom." In *Understanding the Old Testament*, 528–62. Englewood Cliffs, N.J.: Prentice-Hall, 1975.

Atkinson, Brooks. "From 'Job' to *J.B.*" *The New York Times*, 4 May 1958.

Besserman, Lawrence L. *The Legend of Job in the Middle Ages*. Cambridge: Harvard University Press, 1979.

Borges, Jorge Luis. "El Libro de Job." In *Conferencias*, 93–102. Buenos Aires: Instituto de Intercambio Cultural Argentino-Israeli, 1967.

Crossan, John D., ed. "The Book of Job and Ricoeur's Hermeneutics." *Semeia* 19 (1981): 3–123.

Dahood, Mitchell. "Chiasmus in Job: A Text-Critical and Philological Criterion." In *A Light unto My Path: Old Testament Studies in Honor of Jacob M. Meyers*, edited by Howard N. Bream, Ralph D. Heim, and Carey A. Moore. Philadelphia: Temple University Press, 1974.

Daiches, David. *More Literary Essays*. Edinburgh: Oliver & Boyd, 1968.

Damon, S. Foster. *Blake's Job: William Blake's Illustrations of the Book of Job*. Providence: Brown University Press, 1966.

Dhorme, E. *A Commentary on the Book of Job*. Translated by Harold Knight. Leiden, Netherlands: Nelson, 1967.

Ewing, Ward B. *Job: A Vision of God*. New York: Seabury, 1976.

Froude, James Anthony. "The Book of Job." In *Short Studies on Great Subjects*, vol. 1, 266–320. London: Longmans, Green, 1867.

Frye, Northrop. *Spiritus Mundi: Essays on Literature, Myth, and Society*. Bloomington: Indiana University Press, 1976.

Ginsberg, H. L. "Job." In *Encyclopedia Judaica*, vol. 10, 112–19. New York: Macmillan, 1972.

———. "Job the Patient and Job the Impatient." *Conservative Judaism* 21 (1967): 12–24.

Girard, René. *La route antique des hommes pervers*. Paris: B. Grasset, 1985.

———. *Violence and the Sacred*. Translated by Patrick Gregory. Baltimore: Johns Hopkins University Press, 1979.

Glatzer, Nahum N. *The Dimensions of Job: A Study of Selected Readings.* New York: Schocken, 1969.

Gordis, Robert. "All Men's Book: The Book of Job." In *Poets, Prophets and Sages: Essays in Biblical Interpretation,* 280–304. Bloomington: Indiana University Press, 1971.

————. *The Book of Job: Commentary, New Translation and Special Studies.* New York: The Jewish Theological Seminary of America, 1978.

————. "The Temptation of Job." In *Poets, Prophets and Sages: Essays in Biblical Interpretation,* 305–24. Bloomington: Indiana University Press, 1971.

————. "Wisdom and Job." In *The Book of God and Man: A Study of Job,* 31–52. Chicago: University of Chicago Press, 1965.

Gros Louis, Kenneth R., James S. Ackerman, and Thayer S. Warshaw, eds. *Literary Interpretations of Biblical Narratives.* Nashville: Abingdon Press, 1974.

Hone, Ralph E., ed. *The Voice Out of the Whirlwind: The Book of Job.* San Francisco: Chandler Publishing, 1960.

Jung, Carl G. *Answer to Job.* Princeton: Princeton University Press, 1973.

Kallen, H. M. *The Book of Job as Greek Tragedy.* New York: Moffat, Yard, 1959.

Kluger, Richard Scharf. "Satan as One of the *bene ha-'elohim.*" In *Satan in the Old Testament,*" translated by Hildegard Nagel, 79–136. Evanston, Ill.: Northwestern University Press, 1967.

Lacocque, A. "Job and the Symbolism of Evil." *Biblical Research* 24/25 (1978–80): 7–19.

MacLeish, Archibald. *J. B., A Play in Verse.* Boston: Houghton Mifflin, 1958.

Newman, F. X. "The Land of Ooze: Joyce's 'Grace' and The Book of Job." *Studies in Short Fiction* 4 (1966): 70–79.

Polzin, Robert M. *Biblical Structuralism.* Philadelphia: Fortress Press, 1977.

Polzin, Robert, and David Robertson, eds. "Studies in the Book of Job." *Semeia* 7 (1977): 1–154.

Richards, Ivor Armstrong. *Beyond.* New York: Harcourt Brace Jovanovich, 1974.

Ricoeur, Paul. *The Symbolism of Evil.* Boston: Beacon Press, 1969.

Rose, Jacques-Leon. "Oscar Kokoschka's Phantasmagorical Vision: The Book of Job Transmogrified." *Comparative Drama* 2 (1971): 91–100.

Rowley, Harold Henry. *Job.* Grand Rapids, Mich.: Eerdmans, 1976.

Saggs, H. W. F. "The Divine in Relation to Good and Evil." In *The Encounter with the Divine in Mesopotamia and Israel,* 93–124. Atlantic Highlands, N.J.: Humanities Press, 1978.

Sanders, Paul. S., ed. *Twentieth Century Interpretations of the Book of Job.* Englewood Cliffs, N.J.: Prentice-Hall, 1969.

Stout, Janis. "Melville's Use of the Book of Job." *Nineteenth-Century Fiction* 25 (1970): 69–83.

Tsevat, Matitiahu. *The Meaning of the Book of Job and Other Biblical Studies.* New York: Ktav Publishing, 1980.

Tur-Sinai, N. H. *The Book of Job: A New Commentary.* Jerusalem: Kiryath Sepher, 1957.

Urbrock, W. J. "Oral Antecedents to Job: A Survey of Formulas and Formulaic Systems." *Semeia* 5 (1976): 111–38.

Von Rad, Gerhard. "Job xxxviii and Ancient Egyptian Wisdom." In *The Problem of the Hexateuch and Other Essays,* 281–91. London: Oliver & Boyd, 1966.

Westermann, Claus. *The Structure of the Book of Job: A Form-Critical Analysis.* Translated by Charles A. Muenchow. Philadelphia: Fortress Press, 1981.

Wiesel, Elie. *Messengers of God: Biblical Portraits and Legends.* Translated by Marion Wiesel. New York: Random House, 1976.

Zhitlowsky, Chaim. "Job and Faust." Translated by Percy Matenko. In *Two Studies in Yiddish Culture.* Leiden, Netherlands: E. J. Brill, 1968.

Acknowledgments

"The Reaffirmation of the Tragic" by Paul Ricoeur from *The Symbolism of Evil* (Religious Perspectives, vol. 17, planned and edited by Ruth Nanda Anshen) by Paul Ricoeur, © 1967 by Paul Ricoeur. Reprinted by permission of Harper & Row Publishers, Inc.

"Blake's Reading of the Book of Job" by Northrop Frye from *Spiritus Mundi: Essays on Literature, Myth, and Society* by Northrop Frye, © 1976 by Indiana University Press. Reprinted by permission of Indiana University Press.

"God under Attack" (originally entitled "The Book of Job: God under Attack") by David Daiches from *God and the Poets: The Gifford Lectures, 1983* by David Daiches, © 1984 by David Daiches. Reprinted by permission of Oxford University Press.

"Truth and Poetry in the Book of Job" by Robert Alter from *The Art of Biblical Poetry* by Robert Alter, © 1985 by Robert Alter. Reprinted by permission of the author and Basic Books, Inc.

"Job's Encounters with the Adversary" by Ken Frieden from *Response: A Contemporary Jewish Review* 14, no. 3 (Winter 1985), © 1985 by *Response: A Contemporary Jewish Review*. Reprinted by permission.

" 'The Ancient Trail Trodden by the Wicked': Job as Scapegoat" by René Girard from *Semeia* 33 (1985), © 1985 by the Society of Biblical Literature. Reprinted by permission of the Society of Biblical Literature.

Index